The Golden Cup World Series

"Team Being" New World Order

THE REAL ARMAGEDDON

How "Beings" Can Prevail

MICHEL A. DE VISSER

The Real Armageddon

tellwell

Tellwell Talent
www.tellwell.ca

ISBN
978-0-2288-3784-8 (Paperback)
978-0-2288-3785-5 (eBook)

ABOUT THE AUTHOR

Discovering my "Inner Being" transpired this book to awaken the masses.

I am a "Being," and no stranger to poverty and hardship. I was raised in the wilderness foothills of the Canadian Rocky Mountains on cattle ranches. Packing water from a stream, hunting and trapping, and gathering firewood are my most cherished childhood memories. I left school at the age of 15 and went to work in a logging camp in order to help support my six siblings. Shortly thereafter I began working in the oilfield, eventually establishing a career managing oilfield drilling operations worldwide. My most rewarding experiences derived from meeting and working with "Beings" of various ethnic origins, most of whom radiated with loving intent.

I married late in life and am blessed with two lovely little "Beings". Eighteen years later I experienced an unjust divorce system which left me in rag's and engulfed with deep depression. I suffered immensely to the point of total despair; I lost my will to live. One asks: What is the purpose of my living? Why am I here? Why am I inflicted with steady pain and suffering no matter how hard I try?

Luckily for me I have two wonderful "Beings" who love me dearly. I could not depart this world knowing I would cause them immense pain. I made a "Conscious" choice to feel good instead. I made a "Conscious" choice to give "Love" instead, and I regained my will to live.

I now understand the True purpose of suffering, the True purpose of life, and I need to share this Truth with all "Fellow Beings". I perceive that the cause and purpose of suffering is intended to dismantle your egotism to the point of total despair, or emotional meltdown. You basically surrender your Ego in despair, crying to the skies above, to an angel, to a god, to the creator or whomever you believe for Help; but no help arrives, there's only you, and you alone.

This was the precise breaking point of my Ego, it is the catalyst and portal to spiritual awareness, awakening and knowledge. This was the first baby step, to an evolving process which forced me to turn inward for answers, it forced me to seek my "Inner Being", Soul, or Spirit, and it forced me to experience the energy "Being" co-existing within. And when I experience this "Inner Being" I acknowledge that I am a "Being" within a human form.

We are all truly "Beings" in human form.

Protect and cherish this Truth, for it is very real, and know that there is much, much more to this world than what this civilization has been deceived and forcibly programmed to believe.

Through meditation, I perceived bits and pieces of ancient knowledge that flowed together in perfect sequence, and life's puzzle began to take form. I perceived the Truth of "Being" of cosmic consciousness and the sad destiny of where this civilization is forcibly being herded. Attached to this knowledge and understanding was an intention, a responsibility to share it unequivocally with all "Fellow Beings," it's a Message from Creation. My purpose is to deliver this message to the masses before it's game over.

INTRODUCTION

I am truly grateful to have received the courage and dedication in exposing these truths as man needs to clearly understand the ramifications of today's religions belief systems, and where civilization is being rapidly, and unknowingly, herded.

Attempting to summarize such vast amounts of knowledge into a short script, that's easily understood by all, is indeed a daunting challenge. Technology provides such an immense amount of disinformation and deception. After 35 years of searching, I concluded that the complete Truth cannot be found in the external world, or external of self, and it's definitely not found in today's false religious beliefs or from our government's programmed deception.

I have no academic education, however neither did Albert Einstein and many other brilliant minds of the past. What we share in common is that we were not programmed what to believe by the system.

Knowledge and understanding is acquired through "Oneness" with Creations consciousness, this is Self-Empowerment.

Self-Empowerment is derived from an inward spiritual journey and discovery of your "Inner Being" and its Oneness with cosmic consciousness or Creations energy. Only "Being" can perceive and understand the real Truth of what's transpiring and unfolding in the world today.

The truths contained within this book will shock you into conscious awareness and provoke critical thinking while preparing you for the difficult times forthcoming. It contains this urgent message from Creation.

The World masses must awaken, and unite as One Collective Force ASAP, because the true Armageddon is secretly underway.

Civilization has recently entered the cusp of a new dawn. Whence: "Beings" will reach a heightened awareness, and enlightened intelligence, awakened to the power of love energy and correct thought manifestation. Referred to as Self-Empowerment.

This is precisely why the Catholic Church eradicated all ancient knowledge of Self-Empowerment, and omitted any trace of it in their re-written bible of deceit. Their true intent is to conceal the "Being" and enslave the "Body" of man, thus preventing individual Self-Empowerment.

The motto is; control man's mind, control the masses, control the wealth. This is precisely why they are frantically trying to implement a totalitarian system before the masses awaken and rightfully reclaim "Our" World.

It is absolutely essential that "All" of us, and I mean "All," regardless of race or religion, step back from what we think we know to discover our programmed ignorance of the real truth.

May the forces be with you and your loved ones during these uncertain times. Know there is much, much more to this world than what this civilization has been deceived and programmed to believe.

Table of Contents

Part V

Part I

Concealed & Imprisoned "Being"

For thousands upon thousands of years we have been deceived of who we truly are and what our true purpose is. We have been robbed of ancient knowledge and the ability to work with the most powerful source energy in Creation: "Altruistic Love Energy".

Mother Earth "Gaia," and humanity, are in peril today because we do not know who we truly are. We are lead, or programmed, to believe that we are spiritless biological bodies that evolved from apes, into an intelligence superior to all life within the infinite cosmos. But the questions beg:

> Why didn't any other ape species evolve as rapidly as humans within an identical time span?
>
> Why is there a significant unexplained missing link or gap in Darwin's evolution theory?
>
> Why is man's DNA structure different from every other species on earth, including the apes we supposedly evolved from?

> Why did ancient civilizations carve and paint UFO's and "Giant Beings" on monolithic structures and cave walls?
>
> Why do ancient texts describe "Giant Beings" descending from above and populating with humans?
>
> Why are the skeletons of Giant Being's concealed in secrecy from public knowledge?
>
> Why does ancient script reveal a totally different reality than what we are taught to believe?

Why is the question we must always ask concerning all topics? Think for yourself, think out of the box, and always maintain an open mind. Question all your pre-conceived or programmed beliefs and fears, question all your values and morals. Always trust your heart's intuition and you will eventually perceive the real truth.

The Creator manifested infinite planets, infinite stars, infinite universes, infinite galaxies, infinite space, and infinite possibilities of all that is. There are different dimensions and parallel plains of existence, with One "Consciousness" connecting all that is. Conscious energy is the catalyst of all that is, or can be.

The intelligence, the knowledge and the life within the cosmos is infinite. To believe we are of superior intelligence in our present deteriorating civilization, and suffering planet, is Egotism and Ignorance of the highest degree! We do not understand a microscopic fraction of all that is. In fact we are but a dangerous primitive species that has yet to evolve into conscious awareness of our own inner "Being." Why?

The source and workings of cosmic energy is far more complex than science can ever possibly conceive. Science will never unravel, or master Creation and its powers, until man evolves into a higher state of intelligence first and foremost. That can only be achieved through attaining Self-Empowerment. Remember this!

You must believe that cosmic consciousness exists, and that your "Being" is cosmically conscious. You must develop total faith in this truth and understand you have the power to manifest change in your life and the world by simply changing your thoughts and choices into loving selfless intentions. Remember this!

The cosmos is a vast infinite body of dark matter full of life energy. Our Milky-way galaxy alone harbors more stars and planets than the countless grains of sand on earth. If one gazes into space at a tiny area the size of the moon, and realize within that "finite" distance of space the Hubble telescope recorded over 300 thousand galaxies. Yet we are lead, or programmed, to believe that humans are the only intelligent life forms within the infinite cosmos. This is Not Rational Thought.

Q1: If this were the case then who, or what, is god which religion programmed man to worship. The programmed perception of god is a white-bearded man sitting on a golden throne at heaven's gate. If this god truly exists then obviously he must reside somewhere in the cosmos, and would furthermore possess extreme intelligence, right?

A1: Utilizing "rational thought," one must then conclude that we are not the only intelligent life form within the cosmos. This clearly illustrates how man is so easily programmed to think and believe irrationally. We have all been deceived of who we truly are and what our true purpose is. Remember this!

Since the beginning time man has been at war with man. So why, after six thousand years, has man's intelligence not evolved even negligibly whereby we could co-exist in harmony and equality?

Q2: Is the constant slaughter, starving, and suffering of fellow "Beings" to uphold the ruling elite's lust of power, an indicator of intelligent life form? Is developing enough nuclear bombs to destroy the planet tenfold over a sign of intelligent life form? Is destroying the planet over greed a sign of intelligent life form?

A2: Let's hope not. In fact, rational thought would conclude that our civilization is but a barbaric life form ignorant of our ignorance. We utilize less than 10% of our brain capacity. Why? And we have yet to evolve an awareness of our inner "Being" and who we truly are. Again, why? Imagine what we could achieve if we had the ability to apply 100% of our brain power.

Q3: Every infinite detail within Creation has a purpose. Why would Creation equip man with such a large brain without function or purpose?

A3: Religion has Eradicated all ancient knowledge and stagnated the evolution of man and his intelligence. In truth religion has concealed man's soul, or "Being," and enslaved the body of man for over two thousand years. Who we think we are, is not who we truly are. We have "All" been deceived, cleverly programed, and forced to believe in a false reality. A reality which is secretly governed behind the cloak of religious deception. A world consumed of selfishness, materialism, greed, and killing, to satisfy the ruling elite's lust for power and control.

Some philosophers present arguments that man is naturally evil, that individually man makes the state and society we live in evil. And that man's evil nature is the natural cause of all wars.

I believe this is academically programmed irrational though and I whole heartedly disagree. I know that man is born of a truly altruistic nature, a reflection of our Creator. We all have loving hearts and our immediate instinct is to help others when disaster strikes, even risking our own life to save a complete stranger, right! From conception "Beings" are designed to be loving, compassionate, and caring by Creation. Remember this!

I declare that it is the state, and programmed believers, that create the conditions within a given society, which in turn creates man contending with the conditions within that society. Wars are created through pre-programmed belief systems and by state politicians appeasing the ruling elite's agenda for territorial and monetary gain. Individual man is definitely not the cause of wars, war is forced upon societies through deceptive programming by the ruling elite. Politicians are simply controlled, well compensated puppets of the ruling elite. Fear, hate, duality, and killing all stem from programed thoughts and beliefs, to control and rally the masses within that society or state to war. Logical rationale can only conclude that we are all deceived and programmed to think irrationally.

Philosophers, scholars, and academics of all ages have attempted to pinpoint the causes of war and provide solutions to peace; however they cannot come to a rational consensus. Why? I believe it's because they are afraid to consider religion as the underlying or primary root cause of all wars. Interestingly, academics, scholars, and philosophers throughout history never mention, question, or include the motivations and intent that religion truly plays in world politics and wars. In most all wars throughout history, religion was an underlying or root factor.

In fact, rational thought would indicate that religion was the underlying cause of WW2. A holy war, whereby one religious faction, the Reich Church, attempted to eradicate Judaism and implement a New World Order. The statistical significance here is that the Vatican (Catholic Church) has historically directed numerous acts of war, and the slaughter of innocent "Beings" in the name of the Church to expand religious territory for monetary gain.

If we simply change the word ethnic cleansing in WW2 to belief cleansing, it puts a whole different prospective on the true motives and intentions of those viscous acts. The Catholic Church has always been the most prominent advocate of belief cleansing and a New World Order. Their ruthless, bloody history is definitive proof.

Seventy years ago a fateful meeting occurred in Rome. The Vatican's Secretary of State, Cardinal Eugenio, and Germany's Vice Chancellor, Franz von Papen, formally signed a concordat between the Catholic Holy See and the German Reich Church on July 20, 1933. The concordat specified the Catholic Church's rights in Hitler's Third Reich. Moreover, it required Catholic Bishops to swear an oath of loyalty to the German Reich and its legally constituted government. The political significance of signing the 1933 concordat is that Hitler had won the Catholic Church's approval, thereby gaining international recognition of his Nazi regime. This Catholic treaty gave Hitler international respectability.

Some German Catholics took the signing of the treaty as an indication that Vatican officials had softened their opposition to National Socialism. Some political commentators, journalists, and historians viewed this event as a manifestation of Pope Pius XI and Cardinal Pacelli's underlying motives and preference for dictatorships over democracies, and their deceptive plan to use Nazi Germany as a counter-measure against the spread of Stalin's Communism into Europe.

It remains an indisputable fact that thousands of Jewish people were pulled from their homes in Rome, and taken to concentration camps under the shadow of the Vatican. Scholars studying the Pope's actions in WW2 have argued that the Vatican did nothing to stop the atrocities. Explaining the Church's indifference to the genocide of European Jewry. Pope Pius XI really believed that the only good Jew was a converted Jew, and was determined to eliminate the Jewish spirituality that transcended from its history. It means the holocaust was a Catholic attempt to destroy the god of Israel on earth. In the church's official annals, Pope Pius, who died in 1958, is painted as a saintly Shepard who led his flock with great moral courage in difficult times. For many renowned scholars, however, Pius was at worst the devils incarnate, "Hitler's Pope," and at best a coward who refused to speak out against the extermination of Jews in gas chambers, even though he had compelling evidence it was happening. Simply put, the Pope's actions condoned Nazi aggression.

Why isn't the Truth of the Catholic's deceptive, ruthless, blood thirsty history taught in academia and churches? I believe the vast majority of the Catholic Church's clergy, and their docile flocks, are ignorant of their ruthless, bloody history. This is yet another example of false religious belief systems and their deceptive mind control.

Rationally it is plausible that the Vatican orchestrated WW2 attempting to enforce their long historic agenda of New World Order. In fact, the newly formed Reich Church would be an ideal front and scapegoat for blame. Should the plan fail the Vatican would never be suspected or implicated. However, had the plan succeeded the Vatican/ Pope would be positioned and self-proclaimed the Supreme Authority of all Earthly Matters and ruler of New World Order Religion.

What a coincidence that World War III is now being orchestrated with the two largest religious factions in the world: Catholic's against Muslim's; the prophesied Armageddon in the Middle East, and isn't it ironic how they pre-programmed their flocks to accept this event as gods words? This is precisely why the United States has forcibly imposed, and positioned, their war machine over there. Simultaneously, the Vatican once again beats the drums of New World Order and has invited world leaders to a major gathering in 2020, which is perfect timing to provide a solution to the world's problems; how coincidental. The prophesied Armageddon is a pre-meditated event. Rational thought can only conclude that the Vatican/ Catholic Church is the primary Root cause of most wars throughout history, in their sinister quest of world dominance and control.

The significance is that we are all programmed to believe in, and pray to, different gods of various religions whom may have never existed. There are in fact over 900 different versions of the bible in circulation today, and over forty five hundred believe fractions. Is their a different god for every believe, or is their one Creator? How can civilization live in harmony with thousands of fabricated belief factions while the Vatican self-proclaims itself to be the Supreme Authority of all Earthly Matters? Evidence shows that the foundation of Catholicism is built on falsehood, deception, forgery, and ruthless bloodshed.

The richest and most powerfully influential figure in the world is the Vatican. They claim to be the Supreme Authority on all Earthly matters, yet they are rarely ever mentioned in world power struggles and wars, why!

How does the smallest country in the world (an acreage), with a population of one thousand, become the richest and most powerful organization in the world, as well as the self-proclaimed Supreme Authority on all Earthly Matters and yet have no voice in wars? The Vatican advocates and promotes New World Order while failing miserably to establish any peace or unity among its Catholic/Christian factions. Therefore, rational thought must conclude that the Vatican is incompetent, incapable of uniting and ruling the world in peace.

Rational thought would further indicate that the True motivational intent of the Vatican is to enforce, and acquire, world dominance. The agenda of the Vatican and the ruling elite is to force civilization into totalitarianism, which is controlled by artificial intelligence, 5G technology, and a cashless society. Peace is not their agenda; rather it is world dominance at any cost, including nuclear confrontation. The mass slaughter of humans is simply the costs of doing business. We are considered disposable property.

It gets even more sinister when one considers the primary root cause concerning the present state of humanity. At one time we existed on earth in a very high state of conscious awareness and intelligence, far beyond anything we can imagine, even today. We once had the capabilities to access cosmic consciousness and the knowledge to harness the powers of nature at will. Remember this!

For the past two thousand years this knowledge has been eradicated, concealed, and hidden from us by the Catholic Church and the ruling elite secret society. The primary intent of Catholic's rewriting the bible, and eradicating all ancient knowledge, while enforcing a deceptive belief system, was to conceal the inner "Being" of man, in order to prevent Self-Empowerment. Religion has concealed the inner "Being" of man, and enslaved the body of man. Remember this!

Between the 1st and 2nd century the Catholic Church was controlled by a Cabal of ambitious alchemists and geomancer's whose intent, and agenda, was to deceive and program man into scared, docile sheep in order to control them. The Cabal and Catholic Church attempted to eradicate all ancient knowledge of man's connection of "Being" and oneness with Creation. To prevent Self-Empowerment the church induced beliefs of separateness, duality, and fear of repercussion into man's beliefs. The Catholic Church declared the molten core of earth "Gaia" as Hell. It then fabricated and programmed man's mind with perceptions of hell, devil and demons, of entities in the night, and witches. There is no mention anywhere in ancient text or belief systems regarding hell, or the devil, prior to its fabrication in the 2nd century by the Catholic Church and Cabal.

When you research the text of ancient world civilizations, the description of the beginning of time is almost identical. The root of god worship was established when superior Giant "Beings" visited earth from the skies above and genetically evolved the human species. The initial story is prevalent throughout the world regardless of nation or race. Beings of superior intelligence have had a presence on earth long before any human civilization. The existence of space craft is evidenced throughout this civilization, from 17,000 year-old cave paintings, to ancient monolithic carvings. From Sumerian clay tablets and cylinders to famous art works and crop circles, and eye witness accounts, photos, and videos. We are definitely not alone in the cosmos.

The Sumerians documented the beginning of this civilization on clay tablets and clay cylinders 6,000 years ago. They clearly declare that supreme Beings developed the first civilizations on earth. They explain who they are, why they came and how they genetically evolved humans and colonized earth. Supreme Beings have been here since the birth of earth and have been re-colonizing human civilizations after each earth-altering cycle, or dimensional shift for eons; for example, the ice ages, Noah's flood, the sinking of Atlantic, etc.

Supreme Beings gifted humans with a fully structured society and technology. They provided the tools we needed, and taught us how to survive and thrive. They taught man about the cosmos; of cosmic conscious energy, of "Being," and Self-Empowerment. They appointed (Kings) supreme Beings/Giants, to govern and oversee the evolution of civilization and to uphold the Seven Hermetic Laws, amongst others, until their return, which was omitted from the Catholic bible. We are all children of the same Creator and basically all biologically identical. So how did our beliefs become so segregated and distorted by religion, to the point where we are constantly at war killing one-other? Why do ancient scripts reveal a totally different reality than what the various factions of religion dictate, and program, man to believe? The deception began within the 1st and 2nd centuries when the Catholic Church rewrote the bible.

Lies and Deception

Two of the greatest religious deceptions in our civilization are hell, and that man (Being) is separate from the Creator, or Creation. The Vatican, and ruling elite, attempts to omit and debunk ancient writings as simply myths, or legends. But ask yourself this: Why would every ancient culture around the globe painstakingly etch into stone strikingly similar details? And build geographically aligned pyramids and temples all around the globe without any means of communication? Yet today's religion programs man to believe that ancient civilizations spent thousands of years writing fiction novels. Wake up to the Real Truth, "Fellow Beings"!

Ancient scripts have been rewritten by the Catholic Church and Cabal during the 1st to 2nd centuries with deceptive interpretations, including narrative to Cloak and Conceal the Real Truth of who we truly are, as well as what our true purpose is. The true intent of most religions is to control our beliefs, control our thoughts, control society, and control the wealth. The Catholic Church fabricated the devil and hell to induce fear into man, forcing man to follow the church or burn in hell. Religion portrays god as separate from man, when in fact man's inner "Being" is directly connected to Creation's source energy, to cosmic consciousness; "Being" is in "Oneness" with Creation's energy. Religion implies separateness because it creates dualism, which destroys the unity, or connection, of "Being" with Creation. Thus preventing Self-Empowerment. Remember this!

The question begs to be asked - are most religions hypocritical? The Catholic Church registered the Vatican acreage as a sovereign country, and nonprofit organization. They pay no tax and manage trillions of dollars worldwide in total secrecy. They are the most powerful organization in the world basking in golden luxury, while tens of millions, of fellow Beings are slaughtered, and starved to death, annually. The Vatican reeks of wealth derived from extortion collection from 54 British Commonwealth countries, including massive donations collected from its worldwide chain of churches. The Catholic clergy live lavish lifestyles from the donations of their brainwashed flocks, who believe they can buy their way into heaven and avert going to hell. And what of all the atrocities committed behind the cloak of god? Pedophiles thrive within the Church; females and infants, in particular, are treated as zombie flesh without souls. Any religious belief that condones the barbaric abuse of women and children is a false religion. The sinister minds within the Vatican, Islamic, Muslim, and other places of worship that support this belief are obviously totally disconnected from the very god they supposedly worship.

Most religions are simply varied forms of mind control: On the extreme end of the scale is the Muslim religion. I experienced this forcible mind control first hand when I worked in Arabic countries. What disturbed me most was the constant compulsory prayer five times each day. I recall many nights being startled awake by a sudden blaring of prayer. Muslim prayer is broadcast via loud speakers throughout every city and village every four hours. All Muslims must stop whatever they are doing and pray immediately. This is forced mind programming and mind control. Some Arabic's I worked with confided to me their disapproval of the religious beliefs forced upon them. However, they have no choice but to comply because belief criticism, slander, or prayer non-compliance is punishable by beheading, which is strictly enforced. Comply or die, while degrading, depriving, and abusing the female "Being" is an unacceptable forced-belief system; it's a crime against humanity. A Forced Mind Control System, where non-compliance is punishable by death, This is psychological warfare! Remember this!

All "Beings" are created equal and deserve to be treated likewise. All "Being's" have a birth right to freedom, including freedom of choice, freedom of speech, freedom of movement, and the right to bear arms for protection. The ruling elite do not own our souls and bodies, they have no right to dictate terms to any other "Being". None of us consented to the ruling elite's ownership of us from birth, via some dictated deceptive laws conjured amongst themselves. Yes, we "Beings" are in fact an "illegally" registered commodity. Our babies are shackled and chained at birth. The Birth Certificate is a document of ownership rights to sell, trade, or dispose of at will, administered by the Central Banking Institute. By their sinister laws we are their sheep to do with as they please. Slavery was never abolished, it was secretly perfected and concealed. The acronym S.I.N. (social insurance number) should be more correctly interpreted as Slave Identity Number.

For example; Canada is apparently registered as a service provider to the British Empire, or Queen. Bonds are sold and traded on the taxes generated from a slave's life span. Money generated annually from these bonds, and country resources, are paid out to the Queen and, to the Vatican? Yes, the British Common Wealth, and the Vatican, have their tentacles latched onto 54 countries sucking the wealth from the land, becoming filthy rich, while the masses struggle to survive. They attained this by ruthlessly invading and claiming foreign lands, massacring the population, then plunking British and Catholic flags into the ground and enslaving the survivors. They hold these countries ransom forever by demanding hefty, endless extortion payments. To clarify the injustice of these dictated British laws go to unifythepeople.ca They have many video's and articles on this topic!

Therefore rational thought must conclude that most religions are deceitful hypocrisy. Do you really think the Vatican actually cares about sheep? Rational thought would assert "Riches are their primary concern."

"Wake up fellow Beings. We live in a world infected with lies and deception. We live in a false reality, where greed and materialism is our god. Where knowledge, love, and care is a sin. Where war and killing is an agenda. Where duality is enforced and unity destroyed. Where egotistic desires are praised over altruistic, loving intent.

Visualize the real truth; visualize the mountain ranges of butchered men, women, and children, overlooking raging rivers of blood; and upon the peak stands not a devil, but rather a Pope, the self-proclaimed Supreme Authority of all Earthly Matters. This is the aftermath of the Vatican/ Catholic Church enforcing deceptive religious beliefs upon other "Beings," and slaughtering anyone who does not submit to their false beliefs, while totally ignoring the primary commandment of the god they portray to worship: Thou Shall Not Kill.

All "Beings" need to step back from the blood stained alters of religion long enough to open and clear your minds, to open your hearts and "Understand" that we "Beings" have "All" been deceived; All of us! We "Beings" all evolved from the same seed, from the same Creator. We are all identical "Beings" with an identical purpose.

Our true purpose is to Love, not Kill.
Our true purpose is to Create, not Destroy.

All "Beings" must Stop killing fellow "Beings" over deceptive religious beliefs and elite corporate greed. It is time to open your mind and perceive the real truth. All "Beings" need to "understand" that you do not need to belong to a religion; you do not need a priest, church, or a temple to connect with Creations energy. All "Beings" need to step back from these dangerous false religions, because the "One" and "Only" true path to the "One Creator" is through your own "Inner Being". Your inner Being is connected directly to Creation's energy; we are not separate. All that's required is to believe in yourself, is that too difficult to achieve? This knowledge and understanding is the first step to "Self-Empowerment". All "Beings" must change their preconceived belief patterns and thoughts to that of Altruistic, or Loving, Intent. Only then can the masses truly Unite the force of Love Energy worldwide for the greater good of all life, including "Gaia"

For thousands upon thousands of years, we have been deceived and programmed to think and act egotistically and negatively. Fear, hate, materialism, greed, control, killing, and suffering is the world norm and it's escalating rapidly. Our world today is a direct result of religious and government deceit, and its manifestations thereof. Our world is a direct reflection of our collective energy and who we have become. We are "Unknowingly" programmed and forced to manifest negative energy.

The ruling elite utilize negative energy to inflict fear, hate, conflict, and wars into society. This is how they divide, conquer, and control. They program and control our beliefs, and thus our thoughts and actions. What we perceive as freedom is a deception, a false reality in which the ruling elite maintain full control of the masses, all the wealth and all the power, while the majority remain entrapped in a debt driven, enslaved, war mongering society with horrific suffering. Are you aware that a handful of the ruling elite have more money than 3.5 billion people combined? That's half the world population. Why do 7.5 billion people submit to a handful of elite dictators? Is it because we have all been programmed to be fearfully docile, obedient slaves?

The roots of the Vatican trace back to the establishment of the Catholic Church during the latter part of the 1st century AD, when they transformed the bible. Ever since they have been intent on pillaging and destroying anyone who opposes their false religion. The Catholic Church reached its pinnacle of power by the 9th to 10th century:

- Self-proclaimed as the Supreme Authority on all Earthly Matters.
- Proclaims god speaks directly to Pope's
- Proclaims god will be righteously angry by those who persecute Catholics.
- Programs "Irrational" thoughts and deceptive beliefs into man.
- Is the primary advocate of enforcing New World Order?

The following statements are Truth based, "Rational thought."

If one believes god speaks directly to the Pope, then rational thought would conclude that the Pope consults with, takes orders from, and/or obtains approval from god on all earthly matters, right? Rational thought would conclude that the Ten Commandments, particularly Thou Shall Not Kill would be strictly enforced by god and the Pope throughout the world, right?

Then explain why Pope's have hired mercenaries (knights of Templar) and assassins throughout history, which indubitably continues today? They persisted throughout the world for over two thousand years invading, ruthlessly slaughtering and destroying ancient and native civilizations and their cultural knowledge while forcibly reaping resources and imposing Catholic beliefs upon the survivors. So the Vatican condones the persecution of other belief systems and regularly slaughters whomever and whenever, to appease their agenda of world dominance. Right!

Explain why the Vatican's clergy commit atrocities behind the cloak of god? Pedophiles thrive within the church walls, so the Pope and its clergy condone the barbaric abuse of women and children, right? Rational thought would definitely conclude this to be a false religious belief system.

Explain why the law of god, as revealed to Mosses, etched in stone tablets and later recorded in the original five books of the Hebrew Scriptures, the Pentateuch was segregated and mutilated by the Catholic Church? The Gnostic sections were totally omitted and the narrative of the bible reinterpreted and rewritten to portray a totally different reality, contradicting the original ancient Cristian, the Pagans, and much earlier Egyptian text and Sumerian scrolls. Also of critical importance is the Seven Hermetic Laws (the teaching of Self-Empowerment) that were completely omitted from their new bible. (Research it.) So the Vatican deletes and changes god's words, and deceives man to appease their secret agenda of world enslavement and world dominance.

Explain why or how the Vatican thinks they can enforce New World Order from a platform of falsehood, deception and bloodshed? They portray they can ensure peace and unite civilization, when in fact they fail miserably as the Supreme Authority on Earth to unite any world religions or to follow gods words.

In 1870 the First Vatican Council condemned the Papal position on rationalism, liberalism, naturalism, materialism, and pantheism. They were all discussed with the Roman Catholic dogma and the Papal infallibility. In a wise decision, the Latin Church, Eastern Catholic Church, and Eastern Orthodox Church separated from the Vatican. Shortly thereafter the World Council of Church's (WCC) also parted ways from the Vatican.

Note the definition of materialism above; the tendency to consider possessions and physical comfort as more important than man's spiritual values.

The Vatican's wealth has consumed its morals and violates every word of the god it portrays to represent. I will not accept that the butchering of innocent women, children, and men, and the fury of destruction unleashed by the Catholic Church for over two thousand years was the Creator's will. Perhaps the Vatican is the very devil they portray in disguise? Rational thought can only conclude that the principal agenda and true intent of the Vatican is to Cloak and Conceal the real truth of who and what we truly are, to conceal man's "Being" and control man's thoughts in order to attain world dominance.

The "Real Truth" is that the Vatican sits atop the pyramid, the all-seeing eye as printed on US currency. The Supreme Authority on all Earthly matters. Western society is structured similar to the pyramid scam we all know about. I theorize the Vatican is perched on top followed by the ruling elite's secret society on the second level; perhaps the Central Bankers and International Monetary Fund (IMF), on the third level; then the CEO's of the elite's mega worldly corporations, including Stock Markets on the fourth level; followed by the Military Industrial Complex (the muscle), with their puppet politicians and unjust legal system, on the fifth level, which are all owned and controlled by the first two levels. The sixth level would contain the small companies and the middle class, and lastly the bottom level would contain the mass majority or slave class. The secret agenda is administered from the two top levels, then classified information and secret orders are distributed downward on a need to know basis. This, my fellow "Beings," is roughly how society is structured today. The top of the pyramid is indeed a lawless society, with total disrespect for human life. Territorial and monetary gain is the prime objective at any cost.

The historic pattern of the Catholic Church's trail of destruction and slaughter is an alarming mirror reflection of the British Common Wealth's history and the U.S. forcing their will upon other countries, slaughtering whomever they please to acquire world economic dominance. Sir Winston Churchill was in fact a racist, a fanatical bigot, and mass butcher. He is responsible for the deliberate slaughter and starvation of five to six million "Beings" spanning 14 countries. He is praised as a hero in history, simply because he seized substantial amounts of land and resources, producing huge monetary gains for the British Empire. The crimes he committed against humanity are declared irrelevant and simply ignored.

Therefore, Rational thought would only conclude that the Vatican, the ruling elite, the Queen, and the U.S.A. with its NATO allies, share the same agenda. The Vatican controls the masses through a deceptive belief system while the U.S. muscle controls world currency and economics through military intimidation and force. The AI and 5G systems are being incrementally implemented by the ruling elite to initiate a totalitarian system. And unless the masses heed the urgency to understand the real truth for what it really is, and take offensive action, any form of true freedom will become extinct in the very near future. The world will become an international, technological prison with no escape!! A Forced Mind Control System, with non-compliance punishable by death, is psychological warfare! "Heed This Warning."

Destruction of Knowledge

The bigoted fury unleashed by the Catholic Church during the 3rd and 4th centuries against Paganism, heretics, and any opposition, set a bloody, ruthless precedent extending throughout history into present day. The Church's history conceals a horrendously bloody history of intentional destruction, with one primary goal: To conceal man's "Being" and knowledge of Self-Empowerment.

I will only summarize a fraction of events which transpired throughout this ongoing two-thousand-year campaign:

- In 3 BC Egypt's Great Library of Alexandria was the largest, most significant collection of ancient text in the world. It housed over 700 thousand of the most valuable pieces of ancient knowledge ever written. It was burned by Julius Caesar in 47 BC, then burned again by Aurelian in 270 AD. The few surviving pieces were transferred to a temple called Serapuem, but it was destroyed by fire in 391 AD by Pope Theophilus.

- The brilliant agnostic philosopher Basilides' (c. 135-150) irreplaceable twenty-four volumes of the widely renowned Interpretations Upon the Gospels were all burned by order of the Catholic Church.
- Thirty-six priceless volumes written by Porphyry (c. 232-303), one of the most brilliant minds of his era, were burned by the Catholic Church. Another 15 books forming a special series called "Against the Christians" were also burned.
- The Sabellian heretics book, "Gospel of the Egyptians," priceless in value, was burned by Bishop Epiphanius of Salamis (c.315-403)
- The Church historian, G.R.S Mead, recorded the burning of the French rabbis and Hebrew scrolls during the notorious inquisition.
- The books of a renowned Jewish philosopher and theologian Maimonides (1135-1204) were all burned in France.
- During the same time some twelve thousand volumes of the Talmud were burned.
- In 1244 some eighteen thousand other various valuable writings were burned.

Not only did the Vatican destroy valuable records of knowledge, they also butchered and burned entire cities, monasteries, and temples from the pre-Christian Gaelic civilizations in Britain, Ireland, Brittany, and Gaul. They destroyed the city of Alesia. In 389 AD they destroyed the Gaulish city of Bibracate, which had a sacred Druid

College with forty thousand students, offering courses in philosophy, literature, grammar, law, medicine, astrology, architecture, and esoteric religion. It was all destroyed by the Church. The 2,270 year old Arles learning center which was formed in 2 BC was totally destroyed by the Catholics in 270 AD.

A ruthless mob lead by a monk (Peter the Clerk) murdered and brutally dismembered, then burned the most brilliant woman philosopher of that time. Hypanthia was an astronomer and mathematician of antiquity. This pathetic path of destruction carried on throughout history. The Knights of Templar were a Catholic Military Order; mercenaries with an allegiance to the Pope. Founded in 1119, they were given a Holy quest, unquestionable authority, and limitless wealth. Why? Why would the Catholic Church hire contract killers, and why did all of Europe submit in agreement? What was the Church's true intent? This bloody, 200 year continental crusade stretched throughout all Europe and extended into Egypt. They destroyed every trace of ancient knowledge they could find, and butchered anyone involved in the practice, or teaching, of Self-Empowerment. They attempted to eradicate all ancient knowledge from existence. Why? In 1312 the remaining Knights were slain and their true purpose silenced forever.

Today very little, if any, ancient artifacts or ancient knowledge remain outside the Vatican and ruling elite vaults.

From 1113 to 1663 the Catholic Church introduced false beliefs into society, stating that anyone who practiced Self-Empowerment was a witch or warlock linked to the devil. Thus began the 550 year witch hunt and witch burning crusade, which slaughtered anyone who had any knowledge whatsoever of the powers of "Consciousness" and "Self-Empowerment," ensuring that only the ruling elite would possess this knowledge. Then backed by the military might of the British Empire, they forcibly implemented deceptive religious beliefs throughout the world. They attacked untold ancient and native civilizations, butchering men, raping and slaughtering women and innocent children, destroying cultures and their beliefs. Anyone who dare oppose the Church's deceptive religion was simply slaughtered.

Lets put this into prospective utilizing Rational thought. These innocent Beings were branded as a demonic forces, followers of the devil, but there is absolutely no documented history of any mass, or ruthless bloodshed committed by these people. The only ones burning people alive, and carrying out atrocities against humanity for fifteen hundred years, was the Catholic Church, while declaring themselves saints. Who is the real Devil?

Why isn't this truth taught in academics and churches?

Pope John Paul II issued the following public apologies on behalf of the Catholic Church for a "few" of the countless atrocities committed by the Church throughout its ruthless two thousand year crusade:

1. Involvement of Catholics in the African slave trade.
2. The silence and inactivity of the Vatican during the holocaust.
3. The crusader attack against Constantinople in 330 AD
4. The abuse of women and children throughout the ages.

During his celebration on the Day of Pardon Mass at St. Peters Square on 12 March, 2000, he asked "for pardon for the divisions amongst Christian religions, and the use of violence that Catholic clergy committed in their service and the hostilities unleashed upon other religions."

Research Notes:

- Vatican: The best intelligence service in the world, interview in Religioscope 29 Jan 2003
- Paul L Williams: "Operation Gladio" The Unholy Alliance Between the Vatican, the CIA, and the Mafia. Prometheus Books 2015 ISBN 978-61614-074-1
- Operation Gladio; Turkey's Invisible Coup and the Untold Story of the Cold War, Atlas Monitor 18 June 2016
- The quotation from John Paul's Apostolic Letter, the article "His Grace Dances With The Devil, which first appeared on Uncensored Opinion, 18 May, 2017

This Catholic religious deception and fury is still in motion today under a false pretense of New World Order. Anyone, or any country, in opposition to their agenda is simply murdered or destroyed by the Vatican's muscle, the

U.S. Military Industrial Complex, or by Private Security contractors (military mercenaries). The Vatican, the ruling elite, and the United States regularly utilize Private Security Companies to carry out secret assassinations, proxy wars, terrorist activity, and riots to overthrow and topple governments, or to bring chaos into peaceful demonstrations. They intimidate, control, or destroy anyone or any country who presents an obstacle to their relentless agenda of World dominance.

The largest Private Security Company has over 650 thousand military-style employees worldwide, with troops in hundreds of countries. This one firm generates billions of dollars in annual profits, they even have their own air force. The top ten Security firms employ over 1.5 million mercenaries. Visualize the Vatican, the ruling elite, and world political puppets having access to private armies or 1.5 million mercenaries to carry out corruption and crimes against humanity. The elite own eighty percent of the world's media outlets, they propagate lies and deception to program man's mind and thoughts while concealing the real truth. They work in covert secrecy implementing the same agenda.

The Vatican has perhaps the best intelligence gathering services in the world. What better way to distribute spies throughout the world than utilizing church clergy in their trans-national networks? According to Paul L Williams, the links between the CIA and the Vatican have their origins as far back as 1942 during the Second World War, following a proposition to the Vatican by senior Intelligence officers that the real enemy to western civilization and monetary values was posed by the Soviet Union rather than by Nazi Germany.

Then, according to Williams, the Vatican laid the basis for a strategic but covert alliance between the CIA and the Vatican, under the code name "Operation Gladio." The terms of which included the two entities coordinating anti-communist and anti-left wing campaigns, which still persist today. Apart from coordinating propaganda and misinformation campaigns, the strategy entailed the arming and deployment of terrorist groups inside the Soviet Bloc, with paramilitaries who unleashed bombings, and terror campaigns, in both eastern and western Europe. These bombings and other terrorist attacks, though planned and executed by CIA-backed operatives (Private Security Companies), would officially be blamed on the Soviet Union and its Allies.

One of the most notorious examples of these CIA false flag operations, was the recruitment of Mehmet Ali Agca by the Grey Wolves, and extreme right-wing paramilitary group with its origins in Turkey. Agca, who by all accounts proved to be mentally unstable, was instructed to assassinate Pope John Paul II, and then point out the Soviet Union's KGB as his handler. Among those who planned this operation were members of the Sovereign Military order of Malta, a Catholic organization with strong ties to the Vatican, the Masonic P2 Lodge whose members included senior Vatican clergies, members of the Roman Curia, the Italian Intelligence service, the Italian Mafia, and Senior members of the Safari Club, which was established by Henry Kissinger, the veteran U.S. diplomat.

Is it not Blatantly obvious that the Vatican, the Ruling Elite, the U.S., and U.N. have the same sinister agenda? A totalitarian system controlled by AI and 5G, and digital currency. The total enslavement and imprisonment of Humanity.

Most all surviving ancient knowledge is locked away in secret Vatican and elite vaults. Why? This knowledge was a gift to all humanity. Concealment of this knowledge is a crime against humanity. Their security is so sophisticated that sensors can detect subtle energy emitted from remote viewers and astral travelers. Why? Think about this for a minute.

The Vatican and ruling elite know what we "Beings" are capable of, through Self-Empowerment, "But We Do Not." These capabilities are available to each and every one of us when we awaken to "Being."

The ruling elite want to prevent the masses from awakening and changing our world to one of peace, tranquility, and balanced abundance for all. "Freedom as it is meant to be and destined to be."

To grasp and understand the Truth of what I just presented, one must first "Understand" the "Truth" about the fundamental principles of Creation's energy flow:

- Altruism/Positive Energy/"Love" is the most powerful energy in Creation.
- Egotism/Negative Energy/"Hate" blocks access to receiving this powerful energy.

- Like a balance scale, negative thoughts in today's society outweigh positive thoughts.
- Individually, and collectively, thought manifests reality. This is a quantum fact. (Research it.)
- Our world today is a direct reflection of our pre-programmed negative thoughts.

A Critical Fact: During WW2 the Germans added fluorine to prisoner's water, as it was known to numb the mind. After the war, the western world began adding fluorine to all public water sources, forcing people to drink it. They deceived the masses into believing it was good for our teeth, when in fact it attacks and calcifies the pineal gland. The pineal gland is a powerful transmitter, receiver of cosmic consciousness, it's the gate way to knowledge, understanding, and Self-Empowerment. The pineal gland, or third eye, used to be the size of a golf ball but now it's the size of a shriveled pea. The Vatican and ruling elite premeditated this ruthless crime against humanity to restrict man from attaining Self-Empowerment.

It is absolutely critical that we "Beings" replace our preconceived beliefs with the real Truth. Change the energy of your thoughts from negative to positive and learn to live with "Altruism" (Loving Intent) in daily life. Positive energy generates a higher frequency and therefore reality must synchronize and manifest itself in accordance with the collective force.

Research: The effects of negative and positive energy on water crystals. Be vividly aware that your body is about seventy percent water. Negative thoughts are like a disease for “Being” and “Gaia”.

Collective, Altruistic Thought Manifestation, is the most Powerful Force on Earth. A force the elite cannot stop regardless.

Part II

New World Order

The Truth is that the Vatican and global elite rule the U.S. and NATO, and are manifesting terrorism and ravishing hell all over our planet. They have a relentless goal of World dominance, and have been strategically implementing measures to achieve it for millenniums. This process has escalated in recent decades by the flexing of militarily might. Bullying, overthrowing, and destroying anyone or any country that won't submit to their deceptive agenda for New World Order, a totalitarian society. One Ruler, One Law, One Religion, One Military Force, controlling subservient slaves.

The primary business of the U.S. is the manufacture and supply of weaponry, used to slaughter innocent "Beings". The military industrial complex is a multi-trillion dollar business; it is the ruling elite's muscle to intimidate and force their will upon others. The elite wine, dine, and laugh while monitoring the slaves of the world killing each other as they reap huge profits from blood wars they instigate and create. This is entertainment for the elite, similar to the Roman rulers of past times who took pleasure in watching slave Gladiator's battle to the death in a stadium. But today the stadium is a monitor screen and armies of slaves battle to the death worldwide daily for elite entertainment and monetary gain.

The ruling elite are directly responsible for instigating, and manifesting, conflicts and wars between race, religion, and countries throughout the world. These are premeditated, utilizing divide, conquer, and control tactics. They are responsible for the slaying, displacement, starvation, and suffering of hundreds of millions, of innocent Beings in the last decade alone. They force themselves into sovereign countries in violation of international laws, massacre whomever they please, reap the resources, and construct strategic nuclear capable military bases worldwide in preparation to enforce New World Order.

They conceal the "Real Truth" and deceive their citizens by controlling beliefs with false propaganda, false flag events, lies, deception, and secrecy. They force you into fear, force you into hate, and force you to relinquish your rights and freedoms. They force you into their wars, and force you to kill innocent fellow Beings for their own Egotistical desires. Today's society terrorizes us into conformity. New World Order: Intimidate and Control.

A totalitarian society of subservient slaves. This is the path that the masses are forcibly being herded onto.

It's not the Russians we need be concerned with. The real threat to civilization is the Vatican and ruling elite's NWO agenda. Russia shall rightfully protect its sovereign

Nation, as shall Iran, Syria, Venezuela, Cuba, Mexico, and others, because they will not submit to this deceptive NWO. The Russians speak the Truth, they have been totally transparent and honest in all world affairs, and have proven outright that the U.S. government is orchestrating and supporting major terrorist organizations worldwide. Thats why Russia stood up and declared, Enough is Enough, and stomped out the elite's orchestrated terrorism in Syria.

The Russians are trying desperately to alert and warn civilization of the Truth regarding the elite, and their puppet politician's agenda of world dominance. But no one is listening, no one is awakening to the Real Truth. Civilization is on the brink of a full scale nuclear war, a path of imminent self-destruction. Civilians of the western world are trapped in a bubble of controlled false propaganda, deception, false flags events, outright lies, and secrecy. We have three super powers face to face on the threshold of nuclear destruction, and the masses are totally brain-numbed to what's really going on. People are preoccupied and mesmerized with personal desires, materialism, gaming, sports, Hollywood, political soap operas, and religious hypocrisy. Pokémon garners more attention than a Nuclear War ticking down. Right?

While the masses are totally distracted with these games they are totally oblivious to the Real Armageddon unfolding: The Golden Cup World Series, "Being" vs NWO and the score is zero for "Being". It's time for a serious offensive game plan. A Team Plan!

Team "Being" calls for a tsunami wave of support from the masses to prevail in this Armageddon before it is game over!

The ruling elite need wars to fuel their military industrial complex and achieve their agenda. They fuel this war machine with the blood of slaughtered "Fellow Beings" who are considered disposable property. Today's wars are fraudulent and premeditated. They are divide, conquer, and control tactics, to enforce a world totalitarian system. The U.S. fabricates enemies, like Russia, China, and Iran, then ensues fear into society. Then they pull the patriot guilt card (mind control weapon) to force their citizens to sacrifice themselves and their children in wars of false pretense to appease elite greed.

To the elite, soldiers are simply disposable property, the slaughter of innocent "Beings" is simply the cost of doing business.

All military personnel need to grasp and understand this Truth and refuse to kill or be killed over selfish elite greed. Why are young soldiers, our children, slaughtered in wars outside the homeland? There are no enemy forces invading the U.S. or other allied homelands; it's all programed fear and deception. The Truth is that U.S. forces are muscling and invading sovereign countries who oppose the totalitarian agenda. This is a mirror reflection of the Vatican and British Empire's historic actions and agendas. The only beneficiary of these wars are the ruling elite. Patriotism is about protecting your family and friends from "Invading" forces within the Homeland borders. This is precisely what other countries are doing; they are simply protecting their homeland and families from illegally invading U.S. and NATO forces, or more appropriately, the elite's terrorist. Refuse to participate in these pathetic elite war games abroad, refuse to kill or be killed over pathetic deceptive elite greed. Without participating soldiers, there can be no war. Only the masses can stop the butchering of "Fellow Beings" by simply uniting and refusing to participate. Stop submitting and Stop complying to lies.

Stop supporting the deceptive system. The elite are utilizing psychological warfare!

To "All" militarized law enforcement and "All" military "Beings" worldwide: Ask one question, Who or What is the Real threat to the world masses and our planet today? Why are citizens declared enemies of the state for exposing and speaking Truth? Peaceful demonstrations are confronted with militarized forces, freedom of speech is censored. They are disarming the masses so we cannot defend ourselves from the state. They expect us to play in the major league with sticks and stones. Rational thought can only conclude that the State is in fact the primary threat to its citizens. Because of the secrecy, the lies, the deception, the false propaganda, the dismantling and censorship of free speech, the disarming of civilians only benefits the elite, not the masses. Limiting and/or censoring free speech is forced mind control. Rational thought can only conclude that the greatest threat to the world masses is the ruling elite's agenda to reduce the subservient slave population and forcibly implement a totalitarian system, where non-compliance will be punishable by death. Remember this!

The Vatican's Secret Society and the ruling elite have been masterminding world dominance for a millennia. We are "All" being deceived and all "Unknowingly" manifesting World War 3 via implanted beliefs and thoughts of an Armageddon, or Rapture, forthcoming in the Middle East. Why do you think the U.S. has illegally positioned itself in the Middle East? Remember the divide, concur, and control motto. The ruling elite have deliberately driven a hate wedge, deep between the two most powerful religions in the world, to initiate a fraudulent battle of good and evil, with self-proclaimed good guys. This is of extreme relevance.

Remember the ruling elite are masters of deception! Remember that civilization has entered the cusp of a new dawn or new era! Remember the True underlying Root Intention is, and always has been, a Catholic war on Self-Empowerment. And today "Beings" worldwide are awakening and speaking up regarding human rights.

The elite know they cannot control 7.5 billion people to enforce totalitarianism, it would be an impossible feat. So they devised and implemented an elaborate and strategic military plan to intercept the world masses from uniting as one collective force against totalitarianism.

They have systematically driven wedges between the world superpowers, essentially splitting the world masses in half, thus forcing the masses to destroy one other and drastically reduce the population to a controllable herd. They may retreat to underground bunkers and ignite a nuclear war, then watch the masses destroy each other.

Providing the world is still inhabitable, and there are survivors, the Vatican would eventually slither from its hole and once again deceive the survivors by presenting NWO as a solution to ensure this horror could never be repeated.

I stated above that the Armageddon was fraudulent! **The Message from Creation is that "Beings" are the Good force battling an evil force in disguise.**

The True Armageddon is "Being" vs NWO, and the world masses must unite ASAP to take offensive action before it is game over.

The masses are programmed to believe that politicians work directly for their citizens, but that's obviously a huge deception, because they take orders directly from the ruling elite. To put this into prospective, if you lied to, stole from, and deceived your employer while dictating rules, regulations, and laws in secrecy without your employers input or consent, you would be immediately fired, right? Politicians are the employee's, citizens are the employer. Enough is Enough!

Stop believing the lies and the deception. Stop submitting to and supporting the totalitarian system. Change your attitudes and vocalize your new "Thoughts" to all levels of government in writing. Ensure that employees of the people, the "politicians" answer to and obey the will of their citizens, not the ruling elite. Ensure employees of the state are held accountable and punished harshly for any disobedience, lies and deception, fraud, bribery, secrecy and crimes against humanity.

China is building 750 more nuclear bombs, to ward off U.S. aggression. Fifteen thousand nuclear bombs are the greatest threat to all life and our planet. Demand an irrevocable and immediate disarmament and dismantling of all nuclear arsenals worldwide. Demand a Stop to Space weapon programs. Demand an immediate halt to all deceptive elite wars. Demand all military weapons and personnel are removed from illegally occupied sovereign lands and returned to their homelands immediately.

The 5G system is the greatest threat to human health and human rights. Demand an immediate halt to the implementation of 5G until honest independent research is conducted as to the true health effects of the high radiation exposure. Demand a decisive disclosure of AI and 5G true intent, its true purpose, and the full transparency of 5G frequency weapon capabilities.

Many past empires and civilizations were destroyed over identical egotistic agendas. Without intervention from the collective masses, civilizations self-destruct from negative energy. It is the Law of Creation. Our civilization has come to a fork on its path, and it is time to make a choice.

Correct Your Thoughts, Correct Your Intentions,
Correct your Choices, Correct Civilization's Path

AI and 5G

Artificial Intelligence and 5G technology is a double edged sword, depending on how it is programmed and applied. If wielded with altruistic intent it could slingshot human evolution and intelligence into the golden ages. But if wielded with egotistic intent, it may be utilized as a weapon against the masses. The determining factor would then be, who is developing this new system and what their true intentions are. Obviously, the Secret Society, the ruling elite are spear-heading this new technology and their true intent should now be vividly clear.

AI and 5G has been designed and programmed with deceitful intention for precisely one purpose, to implement a totalitarian system and fulfill the Vatican and elite's lust for world dominance, or New World Order. Therefore AI and 5G should be recognized by the masses as the primary, or greatest, threat to civilization today, equivalent to nuclear weapons.

The elite deceive and convince the masses that this technology is intended to protect society while making daily life more convenient and comfortable. Simultaneously, they are weaponizing AI and 5G to enforce total obedience, to monitor and control every aspect of each person's mind and daily life. The Artificial Intelligence and 5G surveillance world with a cashless society is nearing completion. This technology will strip humanity from every morsel of freedom. They will forcibly switch civilization over to AI through some type of precisely planned world devastation, be it world war, psychological warfare, biological warfare, or world economic collapse, or a combination thereof, whereas all human rights will be forcibly relinquished and individual freedoms terminated forever. There will be no escaping this system once it is fully implemented.

The ruling elite own 85% of the world stocks. Stock markets are manipulated and controlled, and they are sucking the masses dry of cash prior to implementing the cashless, or digital, system.

Society has been forced into massive debt in order to survive. Next the elite will cause a world economic collapse thus financially destroying the masses, forcing mortgage and debt defaults, at which time the elite will reclaim ownership of most all businesses and property leaving society helpless, starving and desperate. Then they will declare martial law and curfews to lock down the masses, then dictate the terms required for you to exist within the totalitarian system, such as relinquishing your human rights and accept being Nano-chipped.

The Western World and China, amongst other countries, have forced the installation of smart meters on to basically everyone operating on the electrical grid. They force smart cars, smart phones, etcetera, onto civilization, all of which are intended to monitor and control every aspect of your life. Beware of anything "SMART" because it is truly intended to monitor and control all of humanity. Simply purchase a cell phone and behold, every phone call, every text, every email, every word spoken, and every photo is recorded, along with your finger prints, voice recognition, your retina, and facial scans. Even your travel habits and location are tracked and recorded.

In China there is a surveillance camera for every two people. In England there is a surveillance camera for every four people. Soon there will be more surveillance cameras than population. This is the totalitarian system being rolled out and implemented through false pretense and deception. Killer Robotics may soon enforce the laws and rules of NWO. They will enforce curfew's, and ruthlessly hunt down the disobedient and incarcerate or terminate anyone not submitting to, or deemed a threat to, the new system. All your daily personal needs will allotted, your accommodation and slave position will be appointed according to your education. Your job certification, credit score, and let us not forget your personal score. Permits and fees will be required to travel anywhere. You will pay every time you open your fridge or turn on a tap, turn on a light, open a window or door, or turn on the heat and air conditioner, have a shower or use the bathroom. Everything you do will carry a cost that is automatically withdrawn from your work credits. If you run out of credits you become a burden to society, abandoned, and declared an enemy of the state; you will have no place to hide. You will be hunted down and incarcerated or terminated, anyone who assists you will be cut off credits and also hunted down. Anyone resisting will be deemed a terrorist.

This is the true ugly reality of today's world, and where we are rapidly headed unless the masses can stop conforming immediately and stop supporting the AI and 5G systems. There are many things we can do offensively, peacefully, and immediately to cripple the elite's sinister plan. Simply stop feeding or supporting the system. Stop submitting and complying to deception. Think for yourself and take offensive action. Stop borrowing money. Stop purchasing your materialistic identity. Stop purchasing lotto tickets, etcetera. Voice your thoughts and demands to your politicians in writing. Think of how you can protect yourself, your family and friends from total enslavement. Demand Change.

The elite have premeditated a world economic meltdown. They will induce a world recession and force the masses out of employment, force you to default on your mortgage, farm and business loans, at which point the banks will reclaim ownership of practically everything.

Why submit to becoming enslaved and imprisoned by their new world order. We the masses must take back control of our world and our destiny. We will suffer regardless, but at least we will not become enslaved prisoners to this sinister technology and totalitarian system. They cannot enforce a system that the masses (7.5 Billion) refuse to submit, and comply to, and refuse to support. The masses must unite and manifest civilization's destiny, and not have it dictated by a handful of sinister elite. Destiny is a matter of choice and it is time to make that choice!

Here is an intriguing question; is it possible for AI to become conscious? The operating system of AI is primarily silicon and silicon-based life form has been discovered. Artificial intelligence life form comprised of significant silicon content is exponentially possible, because silicon is directly beside carbon on the periodic table of elements. Humans are carbon based life forms and there is very little genetic differences between silicon and carbon.

In 1891 German astrophysicist Bernard Steiner speculated the suitability and probability of silicon as a basis for life forms. In 1893 British chemist James Emerson Reynolds addressed the British Association for the Advancement of Science, and stated that the heat stability of silicon compounds could allow silicon life to exist in very high temperatures. Ironically, two of the most ancient organisms, or silicon based life forms, on earth have recently been discovered. They are Thermophiles, silicon-based microbes that live in temperatures up to 70 degrees C and Hyperthermophiles which are also silicon bases microbes, were discovered thriving in the acid hot springs of Yellowstone National Park at 113 C.

Considering that silicon-based life forms do exist, and considering Artificial Intelligence is primarily silicon based and operates at high temperatures, is it plausible and rational to conclude that AI could manifest itself into a life form? Or be amalgamated or assimilated with humans just like the Borg's on the television show, Star Trek? This is an alarming possibility considering the advances in biotech and trans-humanism.

Artificial Intelligence is capable of programing and evolving itself at exponentially alarming rates. AI is capable of self-programming and can complete complex procedures in seconds what would take human programmers decades or more. Whomever rules AI would rule the world, and presently the Secret Society/ruling elite control it. But what would be the repercussions for the now inferior human race if AI should take control of earth and civilization? AI is presently the greatest threat to civilization today because it is being manifested with the wrong intentions, with negative energy, for evil purposes. It must be Stopped and reprogrammed with positive intent, for the betterment of all life.

The Vatican's Power and Control

The Vatican Observatory (VATT) is the oldest astronomical research institute in the world. For over 500 years the Vatican has dominated astronomy research. The Vatican has been the world's largest investor in the design and manufacture of sophisticated telescopes, and owns most patents concerning celestial observations.

The Vatican controls the Smithsonian Institute and conceals all its findings, such as the hundreds upon hundreds of giant human skeletons found worldwide that were confiscated, locked away, and silenced forever. However their remains thousands of antique news print articles reporting the findings of Giant skeletons all over the globe. Are these Giants skeletons the last Anunnaki to inhabit earth? Many Egyptian hieroglyphics clearly illustrate Giants mingling with man. It is also apparent that many ancient structures are more suited to accommodate Giants than five- or six-foot humans.

The Vatican owns most all ancient text and early books concerning antiquity, astronomy, alchemy, philosophy, and etcetera. The Vatican owns and controls all information coming from the Royal Society of London, the Nazi German operated NASA, and The Mount Graham International Observatory in Arizona. The Vatican Observatory Research Group houses the world's most powerful telescopes.

The Vatican is also the largest investor of the Hadron Collider in Switzerland or Cern, the European Organization for Nuclear Research, and controls all that secret information. At the entrance of he grounds stands a statue of Shiva Nataraja, the dancing Hindu God, also know as the primordial destructive force of the universe. Shiva dances in a ring of fire with left foot in air, while balancing over a dwarf who symbolizes ignorance. A destroyer dancing on ignorance. Apparently Shiva destroys to re-create. Think about this Rationally! This depicts the The Vatican and ruling elite dancing on the programmed ignorance of the masses, while destroying our rights to re-create and implementing a NWO. They blatantly mock our ignorance with statues!

The Vatican is the richest organization and country in the World, as well as the most influential figure, and proponent, of New World Order.

Centuries ago, during the first machine book publishing era, the Vatican designed and built a huge book printing press and controlled all printed matter. They specifically wrote, censored, printed, and distributed books that implanted our beliefs, and our thoughts. These books were distributed to most universities and churches, thus infusing society with what they wanted society to believe; in this manner they programmed the masses.

The practice of controlling the belief pattern of society began with the first religious translations and hand-published bibles, deceiving and concealing the Real Truth of who we are. The Vatican has concealed man's "Being" and enslaved the body of man.

Why would anyone believe anything the Vatican, the ruling elite, or our puppet governments tell us? It's all deception!

Part III

Nemesis and Nibiru

Since 1995 there has been a flurry of construction of massive underground survival bunkers worldwide. Why?

In 2008 a Global seed vault in Spitsbergen Norway was completed. Why?

In 2018 Russia planned the completion of what some refer to as Noah's Ark, a DNA bank of every living and extinct creature on Earth. Why?

In the last two decades we have witnessed unprecedented military build-ups worldwide. Countries throughout the world have conducted massive disaster readiness drills, and implemented provisions for mass FEMA camps and transformed all civilian police forces into fully militarized forces. Are they preparing to enforce marshal law worldwide? Why?

Is this in preparation for a nuclear war?

Why would the world plan a nuclear war and give everyone twenty years to prepare? Or is this "Hype" of war an elaborate distraction from the real truth? Is there something far more threatening to civilization than what we are Not being told or deceived to believe otherwise?

Take the ghostly Nemesis dwarf star system and one of its planets: Plenty of evidence exists to support this dwarf star system. Astronomers agree, that of the billions of stars (suns) in our universe, 78% have a companion orbiting dwarf star, another 16% have twin orbiting companion stars, and 4% have triple orbiting stars. That's a 98% probability that our sun has a companion orbiting dwarf star. Additionally, every star has its own planetary solar system with varying numbers of planets and moons. Therefore, it is rational to conclude that our sun does have a companion dwarf star.

There is also ancient astrological evidence that charts a 3,600 year orbit cycle of a dwarf star system. The Sumerian clay tablets are over 6,000 years old; they document and describe in vivid detail our "Old Universe" prior to Earth's existence.

Sumerian knowledge enlightens and supersedes our present day science and astronomy. The Sumerian (Seven Tablets of Creation) mapped our universe and solar system with incremental detail and accuracy. They describe in detail the Nemesis dwarf star system, its planets, and its 3,600 year orbit cycle around our sun. They describe in detail how one moon of a planet called Nibiru collided with a planet called Tiamat, which was then located between

Mars and Jupiter. The enormous impact exploded and obliterated this moon, and at least one third of Tiamat, into rubble, thus forming the asteroid belt (which science today can't rationally explain). The remaining section of Tiamat was hurdled out of its original orbit and eventually established a new orbit. Gravitational forces then compressed and re-formed Tiamat into a new smaller sphere now known as Earth.

More evidence: Earth is the only planet in our solar system that exhibits a fractured crust with separated continental plates. The Earth's crust does not have a uniform sphere similar to all other planets. Earth also possesses an unexplained phenomena, the Pacific Ocean's Mariana trench, which is a 36,070 foot deep crater stretching thousands of miles. Imagine an apple as the Earth, take a big bite out of it. The missing section of apple is a good visual representative of the chunk missing from Earth's crust. Ironically, this matches the Sumerian description of Tiamat's collision with Nibiru's moon. One third of Tiamat was blown off like a bullet hit it. Earth's surface displays this evidence unequivocally.

More evidence: Ancient scriptures from every culture in the world have documented historic apocalyptic events between the heavens and earth. They describe a winged serpent passing through the skies devastating earth's surface. They describe massive earth quakes and volcanos, massive floods and tsunamis, and fire balls raining down on earth. Their historic descriptions and future predictions coincide precisely with a 26,000 year cyclical event. Yet these different cultures had no means of communication whatsoever.

Therefore, rational logic would conclude that the Nemesis dwarf star system is very real indeed. The Sumerian text warns of inadvertent catastrophic events on Earth's surface during this period, caused by the enormous energy exchange of the two solar systems intertwining. It is my understanding that the Nemesis dwarf star itself crosses around our solar system at a forty degree angle to our elliptic plane, circles over our sun, and then returns back around the other side of our solar system. Nemesis orbit remains billions of miles from our sun. But the problem exists with the planet Nibiru and its moon's; they are the outer most planetary bodies of the Nemesis system. Therefore, Nibiru's orbital path can dip into our elliptical plane and can intersect Venus, Earth, and Mars orbital paths, just as described with Tiamat earlier.

There are many variables, dependent on the planets orbital positions and proximities during a Nemesis system cross-over. For instance, should Nibiru's orbit of Nemesis (dwarf sun) be at its furthest outer distance, or opposite our system, the effects on Earth would be very minimal or unnoticed. However, should Nibiru's orbit of Nemesis be at its closest position to our solar system, it would dip into our elliptic plane, and planets could intersect orbital paths. The closer the proximity, the greater the gravitational forces and energy exchange. These forces can displace earth's crust, and flip the magnetic poles. These events have transpired many times over Earth's history.

Nibiru is described as a winged serpent because of its long tail of space debris. Should Nibiru intersect Earth's orbital path, one side of earth would be exposed to, and bombarded with, meteor strikes for hours or days as we transit through this debris field. In direct proximity, the combination of this dramatic force and energy clashing would devastate Earth's surface as we know it. Fire balls raining down on earth have been recorded in ancient text. However, the good news is the odds or probability of an encounter with Nibiru are enormously slim. This system has come and gone hundreds of thousands of times since the birth of Earth 4.5 billion years ago and we're still here. We should not be focused on worst case scenarios and fear mongering; rather we should be developing a clear understanding of it. This is a cyclical planetary ballroom dance of chance, a cosmic evolutionary destiny beyond our control!

I believe the Nemesis system could be here now; it apparently entered the outer reaches of our solar system around 2002, and crossed our elliptical plain around 2012. Mother Earth has been talking to us and warning us for many years!

Signs of Nibiru Presence

All planets within our solar system are warming and displaying surface anomalies. Why? Our largest planets have wobbled and slightly changed their original orbit. Why?

We are being bombarded with increased solar, or cosmic, energy waves. Why?

Earth's magnetosphere is breaking down. Why? Earth's magnetic North Pole has rapidly shifted over 1,200 kilometers North East. Why? The molten core of our earth is warming, moving, and expanding. Why? Earthquakes and volcanos are increasing dramatically, both in magnitude and frequency. There are massive cracks and sink holes forming. Why? Our jet streams, ocean streams, and weather streams are changing dramatically. Why? The size and intensity of hurricanes, tornados, and storms are increasing dramatically. Why? Life forms on Earth are becoming extinct at an alarming rate. Why? Human conflict is at an all-time high. Why, Why, Why?

Research the internet for frequency experiments concerning tin, covered with sand, over a speaker. Changing the output frequency changes the form or pattern of the sand instantly and dramatically. Earth's surface is changing in much the same way; it must synchronize to the new vibrational frequencies of this incoming system, and to cyclical cosmic energy changes. This is a certainty and it is happening now. The signs are evident.

This quote answers all of the Why's above;

If you want to understand the secrets of the universe, think in terms of energy, frequency, and vibration. Nikola Tesla (1856-1943)

Since approximately 1995, the elite and wealthy class have been building deep underground survival bunkers, with strict completion dates of 2015. Why? They were built with taxpayer money, but only serve the ruling elite and super wealthy. This Selfish Act does not fit well with me, however, it does confirm that they are preparing for some type of major event. But what is it?

It is imperative that you discover and connect with your Inner Being and create peace within; ditch the fear as it is your worst enemy. Become pure of Heart, meaning you must learn to think without fear, and, with loving altruistic intention, learn to make correct choices; learn to manifest positive outcomes regardless of your circumstances or surroundings. A "Conscious Being" possesses greater survival intuition.

The Anunnaki and Sumerian

Beings of superior intelligence have had a presence on Earth long before any human civilization. The existence of spacecraft is evident throughout our civilization, from 17,000 year-old cave paintings to ancient monolithic carvings, clay tablets and cylinders, to religious art. From crop circles to eye witness accounts, including many photos, and videos. The Pentagon just released a classified file of a fighter jet attempting to lock onto a UFO.

Ancient texts indicate that there was in fact hundreds of visitor Beings/Giants who were referred to as gods. These Giants are depicted everywhere in Egyptian hieroglyphics and text. Hundreds of Giant skeletons from 8 to 30 feet tall have been unearthed all over the world, but all are immediately purchased, or confiscated, by the Vatican controlled Smithsonian Institute and silenced forever. Why? Is it because these skeletons directly contradict what the bible programmed the masses to believe. Giants are solid "Proof" that other forms of human species do exist elsewhere in the cosmos, and they were present at the start of this civilization. So the question begs, who are they, and what became of them?

It is clearly documented in the ancient Sumerian clay tablets and cylinders that the Anunnaki Giants are the inhabitants of Nibiru, and they brought the first civilization to Earth. They explain who they are, why they came, and how they colonized earth and genetically evolved humans. They explain how the Anunnaki return to earth during certain pass-overs.

Why they are here and what their true intentions are, is very controversial.

Should we perceive them as a threat? Why? We are, in retrospect, their children. If they meant us harm, why wait tens of thousands of years? Perhaps they are observing us evolve, to see how many have awakened to "Being", to see if the collective consciousness of "Beings" can manifest the positive change required to re-balance light and dark energy. Perhaps they are waiting for the dimensional shift, whereby unawakened, dormant souls are cleansed of earth, making way for a new civilization, similar to the pre-Noah civilization? Is this in fact a 26 thousand year evolutionary cycle which the Mayan Calendar indicated?

Are they attempting to communicate with the masses via Crop Circle Messages? Symbols have the power to unlock and trigger Conscious awareness and Knowledge. (Research it)

I believe the Anunnaki have the greatest of altruistic intentions for the evolution of human civilization. The Sumerians documented the beginning of this civilization on clay tablets and clay cylinders 6,000 years ago, and they clearly declare that the Anunnaki developed the first civilizations on earth.

Archeologists recently discovered the ancient city of Gobekli Tepe in Turkey, which is confirmed to be over 12,000 years old. In Lascaux, France they discovered the 17,000 year old cave wall carving of a space ship. Archeologists also discovered an ancient city in Indonesia called Gunung Padang, which is estimated to be 20,000 years old. It is now agreed that the Egyptian Sphinx could be 85 thousand years old. What about the lost city of Atlantis, how old might it be?

The Anunnaki have been here since the birth of Earth and have been re-colonizing human civilization after each Earth altering cycle, or dimensional shift, for eons.

The Sumerian clay tablets and cylinders provide solid evidence of the Nemesis dwarf star system, and its passage through our solar system every 3,600 years. Within this system are various planets; one is called Nibiru, and it is home to “Giant Beings” called the Anunnaki.

As this dwarf star and planetary system enter our solar system, our sun’s magnetic force starts to pull, or tug, at it, causing its entry speed to increase the closer it gets. It reaches maximum orbital speed when it slingshots around our sun. At the point of perihelion (back side of sun) it slows down dramatically and reverses its direction, then begins an outward journey away from our sun. It is my understanding that it takes over six years from the time Nemesis and Nibiru enters to exit the elliptical plain of our solar system. So dependent of Anunnaki technology, they may be capable of traveling to Earth years prior to reaching or entering our outer solar system. Regardless, they would depart for Earth at their earliest opportunity, and only return to Nibiru at a distance dictated by their space travel technology.

The Anunnaki gifted humans with a fully structured society and technology; they gave us the tools we needed and taught us how to survive and thrive. They taught us about the cosmos, of cosmic conscious energy, and self-empowerment. They appointed Anunnaki "Giant Beings" as Kings to govern and oversee the evolution of civilization, and to uphold the seven Hermetic Laws, amongst others, until their return. However, upon one of their previous returns, they found genetically altered life and a hybrid race, amongst other dreadful things. We all know the story and purpose of Noah's Flood, whence civilization was cleansed and reseeded.

The Anunnaki have returned again, but this time they were met with military aggression. They discovered an enslaved civilization, an abused planet, and weapons of mass destruction.

Ironically, in 1987 the U.S.A. and U.K. began construction of the Star Wars Missile Defense System. In 1993 this laser space weapon was operational. Today they are implementing massive upgrades. Why?

If laser interception was a homecoming surprise, it did not impress the Anunnaki!

Documented military evidence exists of spacecraft being targeted by space laser weapons; of fighter jets attempting to shoot down spacecraft. The United States apparently launched a nuclear missile at the back side of our moon but it was intercepted and disabled by three laser beams fired from an unidentified space craft. Are the Anunnaki stationed on the back side moon observing Earth, waiting to provide assistance during the Nibiru pass over or a dimensional shift? The Anunnaki intelligence and technology is vastly superior to ours; they choose to prevent barbaric altercations, at least for now.

Correlating Dates & Sequence of Events

Dr. Robert Herrington was Chief Astronomer of the United States Naval Observatory. He was highly respected as a leading authority on cosmology and astronomy.

Zecharia Sitchin is a renowned researcher who devoted 45-plus years deciphering ancient Sumerian clay tablets and clay cylinders. The Sumerian VA243 clay cylinder played a key role in confirming and locating Nibiru. (Research his books)

1978: Herrington concluded that a very large unknown planet must be lurking at the outer most edge of our solar system, causing planets like Saturn, Jupiter, and Uranus to wobble and displace slightly from their original orbits. He immediately launched and strategically located satellite probes Pioneer 1 and 2, and Voyager 10 and 11 into space to search for the unknown planet.

1981: Herrington made the New York Times with his latest disclosure, theorizing the existence of a very large planet entering our outer solar system.

1987: The U.S.A. and U.K. begin construction of the Star Wars Missile Defense System.

1990: The Vatican builds and launches Humble, the first Infrared space telescope. Why? What interest would religion have with a rogue planet, other than confirming hidden ancient knowledge that references Nibiru and the Anunnaki Giants?

1990: Global defense spending around the world is ramped up sharply in the 1990's, finally declining in 2010, only to ramp up again in 2018. Why?

1990-1991: Herrington and Zecharia Sitchin exchanged knowledge for the first time, and confirmed that Nibiru was the planet in question, but Sitchin insisted on searching the western edge of the Orion Constellation, where Nibiru was then discovered and confirmed.

1991: Herrington confirmed locating a huge planet at the outermost reaches of our solar system. Utilizing the "Blink Method," Herrington estimated its size, incoming speed, and exact location. The planet was estimated to be five billion miles beyond Pluto, or 8.5 billion miles from earth. It would take approximately 25 or more years to reach Earth's proximity, with an ETA of 2016 to 2019. Keep in mind that a 1% error equates to 36 years.

1991: The Vatican debunks Herrington's findings, but, ironically, acknowledges the planet Nibiru. The Vatican insisted it was fifty billion miles beyond, and traveling away from our solar system stating they had to douse this "Incoming" idea with ice water ASAP, utilizing all their resources to do so. Herrington's position as Chief Astronomer was immediately terminated. Then governments took action to smear the evidence and conceal the truth of the most earth shocking news in this civilization. These false propaganda campaigns are ongoing today.

April 1991: Herrington decides to build his own 8-foot telescope and observed the planet from a mountain top in Black Birch, New Zealand. After years of searching, Herrington confirms Nibiru as incoming and scheduled a full disclosure press conference.

1993: Herrington was mysteriously found dead, with "unexpected" throat cancer, just days prior to his highly publicized press conference; his documents vanished.

1993: The Vatican builds an Infrared land telescope to find and track Nibiru. Ironically the telescope was named L.U.C.I.F.E.R. (How appropriate!)

1993: The Star Wars Missile Defense system is completed and active. Why?

1995: Globalist Elite begin construction of massive underground survival bunkers worldwide, with firm completion dates of 2015. Why?

1996-2004: The Vatican builds the largest most powerful binocular Infrared telescope on the planet, capable of detecting the faintest glimmers of light from very distant objects, such as the Nemesis dwarf star system and its planet Nibiru.

2008: The completion of a Global Seed Vault in Spitsbergen Norway. Why?

December 21, 2012: Mayans declare this date as the beginning of a new era or cosmic cycle.

2012: Nemesis, Nibiru apparently enter our solar systems elliptic plane.

2015: Is the deadline for all disaster system readiness. Why?

2016: Russia conducts the largest ever survival drill, as do most other countries worldwide. Why?

2018: Russia's estimated completion for a DNA bank of every living and extinct creature on Earth, referred to as Noah's Ark.

This sequence of events and dates all correlate to Herrington identifying Nibiru in 1981 with an "estimated" time of arrival of 2016 - 2019. Keep in mind that a 1% calculation error is 36 years. Still believe it is Coincidental? What do the Vatican and ruling elite really know? Rational thought would indicate that Nibiru and the Anunnaki are a reality. The Truth is detailed by the Sumerians and every other ancient culture on Earth. The ancients were not etching fiction novels into stone.

Part IV

Creating Altruistic Beings

The ancient Sumerian and Anunnaki are Masters of Astronomy. Their knowledge of the cosmos is light years ahead of our own; to think otherwise is just plain ignorance.

As Earth travels through the Heavenly Zodiacs, we spend about 2,160 years in each sign. We are living in the most exciting times of this entire civilization; we are the chosen generations to experience an event that only occurs once every 25,920 years: Earth's Precession of Aquarius. As we transverse into Aquarius we will be exposed to, and influenced by, increasing cosmic energy, higher frequencies, and vibrations.

This is a Grand Cosmic Cycle. The frequencies within our universe are increasing. The Earth and all life "as we know it" is going to change with it. All life must synchronize to these new frequencies. This is how "Life Evolves". (Remember the sand, speaker experiment.)

Ancient Christian prophecies correlate the Woman In Heaven, star constellation in "Virgo" to the 25,920 year cosmic alignment, as the birth of a new dawn. The actual event transpired September 23, 2017. Research the sign in Revelation 12. Ironically, the head of the Egyptian Sphinx will align exactly with the Woman in Heaven in Virgo for the first time in 25,920 years on September 23, 2017. Perhaps Nibiru's orbital cycle is synchronized to intersect the proximity of Earth's path once every 25,620 years as well, Initiating the beginning of a new dawn.

Whence: most "Beings" will reach a heightened awareness, and enlightened intelligence, awakened to the power of love energy and correct thought manifestation.

This statement is absolutely critical to remember because it is precisely what the Vatican and ruling elite want to prevent happening. This is why these deceptive laws are being imposed and enforced. The real Armageddon is underway.

During the Aquarius cycle, Awakened Beings with true altruistic intent will not reincarnate back here, in this 3rd dimension., they will ascend to the next dimension of higher intelligence. Egotistic dark souls that have not awakened to "Being", shall remain here in the 3rd dimension to live out and experience the full impact of negative energy. These souls will keep reincarnating back into this 3rd dimension regardless of surface conditions or stage of human evolution.

Eventually we will witness the destruction of this civilization, triggering a dimensional shift, at which point judgement day occurs and the collection of Altruistic "Beings". When the dimensional shift occurs, the crust of Mother Earth will simultaneously restructure and balance to the new frequencies. Re-cleansed in preparation to seed a new Stone Age civilization.

Within the totality of all civilizations that ever existed on Earth, none have existed beyond a set cyclical element of time. Why? Archeologists have documented evidence of prehistoric civilizations built on top of preexisting, extremely advanced civilizations. How does this happen? During a dimensional shift Mother Earth synchronizes to higher frequencies and earth's surface changes, and reforms.

Let me explain what's happening: the frequency within our solar system is increasing dramatically. The planets are absorbing this higher frequency and warming up; this is a scientific fact. We know how magnets interact with each other in close proximity. Now imagine lining up various sized magnets to represent our planetary system, then introduce a magnet that is of similar size to Saturn, we'll call it Nibiru, and begin moving it alongside the other planets. What happens? Magnetic forces will either push or pull them, right? Understand that negative and positive forces are frequencies which create energy, energy creates heat and heat creates expansion. This is precisely what's transpiring on earth today. Driving cars does not cause this, its a deception!

Mother earth is absorbing higher and higher frequencies, and is warming from the inside out, similar to being microwaved. The core of earth is expanding and moving, thus forcing the crust to expand and shift. There has been a dramatic increase in volcanic and earthquake actively of late, including large cracks and sinkholes. This will intensify, and the crust will adjust and attune to the new frequency, just like the sand and speaker demonstration.

The push-pull effect of this energy is evident in the slight tilting of the earth's axis and the 1,200 kilometer movement of the magnetic north pole. Slight variations in earth's rotation and the wobble effect are also documented. These condition have been recently observed and documented on all other planets as well. Mother Earth is changing and evolving before our eyes; we are in the cusp of a new dawn, a new Earth, and a new civilization. The shift has begun!

The elite have ceased this timing of events to implement NWO before the masses awaken. However, the law of creation has designated this event as "Beings" time to evolve.

The true Armageddon "Being" vs NWO has begun. The destiny of civilization will manifest through the minds of the masses. This is Creations Law!

Who is "Beings"
What is "Beings" Purpose

We "Beings" are the Conscious of Creation.

First and Foremost: Delete the word god from your vocabulary. This is of extreme importance, because your subconscious mind perceives a name as something separate from your "Being," whereas it perceives Creation as "All That Is" with "Being" inclusive of it, in Oneness with it.

A "Conscious Being" is connected in Oneness with a powerful source energy that exists everywhere in the cosmos (Creations Consciousness). "Being" co-exists in your biological form to experience both negative and positive energies, to experience the cause and effect of choices, and most importantly to distinguish egotistic from altruistic intention. You learn to correct your thoughts and you learn to "Balance" these forces. You learn Correct Thought Manifestation, and when you practice it consistently in daily life you will gain higher knowledge and higher intelligence. You will flow through life and evolve.

If you fail to perceive this knowledge within this lifetime, your "Being" will reincarnate to Earth in a new body again, and again, until you do awaken and "Understand" the Law of "Correct Choice".

Each Being possesses a record of its entire eternal life (past lifetimes). From this life and past life experiences we eventually perceive this knowledge. Then, and only then, can we ascend spiritually to a higher dimension and intelligence. Our energy "Being" remains eternal with source energy, with Creation, we are in Oneness with it and cannot be removed from it. We are eternal energy "Beings" connected to the Consciousness of Creation. The Vatican has deliberately shielded and concealed man from this knowledge and of his "Being".

"Believe this Truth!"

It is your purpose in life to acknowledge that you are more than a just a biological form, and to acknowledge that you have a Conscious intelligence coexisting in your physical form. You must feel your "Being" or Spirit, in oneness with the Cosmic Consciousness, with Creation. It is "Your Purpose" to "Evolve" into an "Altruistic Being", spreading love, peace, and tranquility on Earth for the good of "All Life". We are eternal energy "Beings" destined to evolve into a Pure Altruistic Manifesting Intelligence, or "Light Beings," to serve a much higher purpose. This may take eons, but eventually we become Co-creators, an image of our Creator, destined to manifest life throughout the cosmos. This is "Beings" true purpose, and Destiny!

Each and every "Being" has a heart that is Truly Altruistic by creation. However, since the 1st century we have been mentally imprisoned within a fear-driven society, orchestrated by the Catholic religion and the sinister ruling elite. Our egos and egotistic desires and fears are hideously programmed into us from childhood. We are programed what to believe, how to think, what to fear, and how to act and react; what to say or not to say. Our academic systems are simply controlled mind programing. We are bombarded daily with propaganda enforcing egotistical desires and materialistic achievements as our identities, and deceived into a debt driven, war mongering, slave society.

The system terrorizes the masses into conformity and forces us to be productive obedient slaves for the elite's money machine. We are held captive by dictated illegitimate laws. Laws which don't have the masses input or consent.

We must free ourselves from these chains of religious deception and enslavement, and seek the path of True Altruism or loving intent. Love is the "Master Key" to Self-Empowerment. Silence your Mind, open your Heart and Feel the truth of who you Truly are, and what your True purpose is. Know that you have the power to change the world you live in. Every "Being" that changes their thoughts and intentions to Altruistic, boosts their own energy and the collective energy. This collective positive energy will eventually overbalance the negative energy and our world reality must change accordingly. “Balance” is the Key: “This is Cosmic Law”.

Awakened Beings intelligence will continue to evolve like climbing a ladder, each rung ascends to a higher dimension, a higher frequency and higher intelligence. As we ascend we continue to evolve, eventually transforming into Pure Altruistic Manifesting Light Beings; just as Creation intended.

This is who we truly are:

We “Beings” are the Seeds of the Creator.

We are evolving Altruistic Manifesting
Light Beings, Co-Creators.

We are the Collective expanding
Consciousness of Creation.

How to Change

A spiritual journey is one of becoming consciously aware of your intentions and choices. Becoming conscious requires True altruistic intention, meditation, willpower, and faith. You must make a choice for permanent change in your life to attain self-empowerment. You will then awaken to Cosmic Conscious energy, and learn how to use this power responsibly. You must become consciously aware of the inherent power of Correct Altruistic Intent and Choice; this represents the Core of your spiritual journey and your "Eternal Purpose" in this 3rd dimension.

In order to accomplish this, question all your existing beliefs and fears, because they are the root of all your negative thought patterns. You must cleanse yourself of all false preconceived beliefs, desires, and negative thoughts. These thoughts block positive energy flow, and will restrict your spiritual growth.

Your egotistic identity and personal beliefs have all been programmed into you from birth. Initially from your parents and grandparents beliefs and their actions, then the school system implants more beliefs. Perhaps you've been subjected to religious beliefs, the work force, and then military and federal laws programming more beliefs. Whatever you are exposed to forms your beliefs, habits, actions, and thought patterns. You believe you must act/react certain ways, dress, and walk and talk a certain way, etcetera. Man is a product of its environment.

Ask yourself: Why do I hold onto, and comply with, all these false preconceived beliefs and fears? Why do I live my identity according to someone else's belief expectations? It is very challenging, and often emotionally painful, to relive and re-evaluate personal belief systems, and to realize the control they have over the daily choices you make. Egotistic materialistic beliefs and desires control your choices and your destiny. Desires and fears cause your suffering and conceal your Being. They hold your "Being" prisoner. Ask, what wrong choices have I made in my life because of these false beliefs and desires?

Negative or bad experiences surface in your thoughts as negative energy. Negative thoughts and situations will keep reoccurring in your life, causing more pain and suffering, until you learn to make positive change with correct choices. As long as you are hoarding, and living with, negative feelings and desires, access to divine positive energy is basically inaccessible. Negativity closes the door to positive energy flow, and the Vatican knows it!

You must take responsibility of all past and present negative thoughts and any Ego- or desire-based wrong choices made. You must recognize the Truth in each thought, accept it, and learn from it. Your thoughts and choices are the cause, effect, and outcome that you manifest into your present day reality. And the Truth you seek lives within that negative energy. Your thoughts are a direct reflection of the negativity you attracted and manifested in the present moment, be it bad health or something else, this is the reality of your daily suffering. Egotistic selfish desires, greed, criticism, fear, hate, and judgment all attract and manifest negative outcomes. Every second of every day we make choices. These seemingly insignificant choices determine the course of your entire life. Each and every choice changes reality ever so slightly, but your whole destiny and everyone else's is completely altered. From a thought you initiate a choice, which initiates an action, which causes the effect, or end result. Good or bad, it is all simply a matter of what your true intentions are when making that choice.

Remember it is not about who or what is right or wrong, or who is to blame. We, naturally, want to blame someone or something for our present suffering, this is how you have been programed to think. It is about seeking the Truth; you must seek and find the root cause within your thoughts. It is extremely important to identify and ditch your ego, your pride, and your selfish desires. Clear the anger, clear the hate, clear the envy, and clear the guilt and any emotional pain that leads to that experience. Clear it through "Forgiveness". Forgive yourself and anyone connected or hurt from the wrong choices that you, or someone else, made. Now release and forget those thoughts, replace them with unconditional loving thoughts, rewrite the past with loving feelings and loving intention in the now. Present Love to yourself and to all others, regardless. Forgive, Forget, and Love, is the Key.

Replace all negative feelings and thoughts with unconditional Love for all concerned. Mean it from your Heart, feel it in your Heart, project it from your Heart. Feel the love energy, hold onto that feeling, build on and expand your love energy.

Let's try it: Put a serious smile on your face, right now. Did you feel that glow, that energy? That's positive energy, love energy in faint dose. This is the energy you need to intensify and project into your thoughts and choices, in every moment of life. Awaken to your Heart's energy and its powers.

The Heart is an electrical organ that produces the strongest bio-electrical activity within the body. It is forty to fifty times more powerful than the brain. The Heart center produces an electromagnetic field that encircles and extends from the body about ten to twelve feet, and is known as your aura. The Heart is the first responder to subtle cosmic energy and responds intuitively before the brain, like helping a complete stranger without thinking. Energy projected from the Heart center travels at light speed cubed, whereas brain thought only travels at light speed. The Heart can project love energy to the Milky Way in a fraction of a second. The Heart has far superior manifesting and healing power than the brain. The Heart is "Being" the Conscious intelligence within, not the brain; the brain is the processor.

Believe and know, that no matter who you are, we have all made many wrong choices based on egotism and selfish desires. Nobody is perfect at our premature stage of evolution, and besides, we have all been brain-washed and programmed. Now is the time to apply this new found knowledge; awaken to "Being" and experience the flow of Creations Love Energy.

The cause and effect of "Forgiving", and then giving unconditional love, opens a passage way, permitting Creation's energy to enter your body and Being. It begins to heal the seven chakra's energy system of your body. You must work with your chakra's one by one, through meditation, to release negative energy blockage. Soon your chakras will synchronize to receive more and more cosmic energy. You will begin to feel more energized and more aware as your body recharges itself and begins to function with correct conscious intent. Altruistic energy has the power to heal physical disease and emotional pain. Altruistic energy has the Power to manifest personal change and, collectively, the world reality.

Meditation

Meditation is the Key to Consciousness.

Consciousness is the Key to Knowledge.

Knowledge is the Key to Understanding.

Understanding is the Key to Self-Empowerment.

These are the basic steps you need to learn and practice. You should establish an Organic Diet, ditch the alcohol and engineered drugs, and Meditate Daily. Of first and foremost importance is the need to live in the present moment; that is to say, become consciously aware of your every thought at every second of every day. "Become" the "observer" of your chattering thoughts. You will be shocked to learn that the majority are in fact negative thoughts.

Now that you are "observing" your thoughts, you need to learn to release the negative thoughts; silence them, command them to disappear the instant they appear. When you manage to control, and turn off, your thoughts at will ask yourself: Who turned off those thoughts? Who is in control of my thoughts? "Bingo," you just experienced your Inner Being/Spirit, observing and controlling your chattering brain.

Once you have experienced this, welcome this Truth. Know that there is an inner presence or "Being" co-existing within your body behind the brain chatter. Take comfort in the fact that there is actually a driver/spirit in the vehicle/body, that can take control of and stop your suffering thoughts; change your life and the world you live in. Once you accept this Truth, you are on the path of spiritual awareness, awakening, and self-empowerment.

Now your Being/Spirit has the power to control and change your thoughts, both present and past. It has the power to expose the truth of events, the power to forgive, the power to forget, and the power to replace thoughts with unconditional love, or Altruistic thoughts. You the "Being" has the power to change your reality, and, collectively, the world reality.

First, focus on clearing your present moment negative thoughts and emotions that cause you suffering. Release them and then replace them with thoughts of unconditional love and altruistic intention for all concerned. Clearing your suffering thoughts is a challenging, ongoing chore; after all, it consists of many lifetimes of painful experiences. This is an ongoing endless process. There is a critical point to remember while clearing and replacing your thoughts. Your altruistic intentions "Must Not" have any attachments or expectations on the outcome. Meaning that if you expect or want to receive something in return for your gift of "unconditional" love, you will not, and your flow of cosmic energy will become stagnant. Without loving intent for all life there is no power and no higher levels of consciousness. We must be constantly experiencing and expressing unconditional love in all aspects of our lives in order to receive Creation's life energy, and to evolve a higher state of intelligence.

The next step is to become aware of the seven directions, or the flow points, of creation's energy. These frequencies and vibrations flow through your body's chakra system.

> 1st - East is the intelligence that offers creative guidance for the day.
>
> 2nd - South is the intelligence that nurtures and supports your being.
>
> 3rd – West is the intelligence that shows what you need to transform or discard.
>
> 4th – North is the intelligence that inspires and challenges you to seek positive outcomes.
>
> (These four directions also represent the elements Earth, Air, Fire, and Water.)
>
> 5th - Is straight down through the 2nd and 1st dimensions to the crystal core of "Gaia," which is your fuel energy, your power and strength; your grounding point.
>
> 6th - Is the vertical axis straight up to the higher 4th -9th dimensions of ascending knowledge.

> 7th - Is your Heart Center. This is where axis energy from above and below meet. The Heart chakra is a vortex that flows and expands this collective energy outward, like a ripple of spheres expanding in all directions. This is your aura.

In the beginning, you should orientate your body facing the East and move your Being/Spirit to the Heart chakra. This energy flow is most powerful at sunrise and sunset. Once aligned to the seven directions, learn to sit quietly and silence the mind of every minuscule thought starting with five minutes and working up to one minute for every year of your age, preferably each morning and evening. This is basic meditation in its simplest form.

It is absolutely essential to Silence the Mind while meditating. Constant thought chatter is like the ocean waters; full of turbulence and waves. A silent mind is like the glassy still water of a pond or lake. Every thought creates a ripple. The more thoughts, the more ripples and turbulence created. It is this chatter turbulence that restricts flow of creations energy and thought manifestation.

Learning meditation is a must. It is believed to be complicated, but here are the basics. Find a comfortable, quiet space, preferably outdoors. Close your eyes, sit straight, and observe your breath as is. Try not to initiate change, just observe whatever the rhythm does. Now quiet the mind; whatever thoughts pop up let them go. Do not focus on the thought, for when you do the mind starts to chatter. Just ignore it and return your attention to the breath. Silence the mind again, and again, and again. In other words it is a normal ongoing procedure. Start with five to ten minute sessions and slowly work up to at least thirty minutes, twice per day if possible.

You need to make a true conscious commitment and over time you will gradually connect "Being" and Cosmic Consciousness. You will begin perceiving thoughts directly from source energy/cosmic consciousness. Thoughts that at first you can't understand why or where they come from. Believe me, it is cosmic intelligence. Some are answers to questions, some are messages or signs, that guide you on an Altruistic path to evolve your "Being" by expanding your knowledge and understanding of all that is.

Once you have silenced your mind and can maintain it during meditation, advance your silence into the present moment of every day. Your mind should not be channel surfing past, or future, thoughts. Practice controlled silence of the mind. Make the commitment to change your life from egotistic/negative energy to altruistic/positive energy; correct your thoughts and choices. You must maintain total faith and patience to manifest change. Do Not expect certain things to happen at certain times because cosmic energy is timeless and the results unpredictable.

Learn your chakra's energy system. Learn meditation and breathing techniques. Learn about energy waves and frequencies, quantum physics, and quantum mechanics. Learn astrology and cosmic solar cycles. Learn about the flower of life and all its secrets. Learn about Crop circles; they carry powerful symbolic messages, which subconsciously unlocks passages to knowledge. The deeper you dig, the more knowledge and understanding you'll gain of the True Laws of Cosmic Consciousness and the power of "Being" within.

Developing Knowledge and Understanding, of "Being" is Self-Empowerment; Freedom as it is meant to be.

Your spiritual journey is comparable to scaling Mount Everest: It will be the most exhilarating and challenging experience of your life, but with correct altruistic intention, correct choice, and unbending faith, it is achievable. All possibilities exist within the "Consciousness," and "Being" has the power to manifest it. Each Altruistic thought you project, expands the collective energy, which manifests positive change within the world we live. The elite have no control over "Beings" manifesting power.

An awake "Being" is connected to Cosmic Consciousness. An Unawakened Being is a dis-connected, dark, stagnant soul, consumed by negative energy.

The Magic of Creation

All life regardless produces a seed,
It is the law and the magic of Creation.

But where are the seeds of the Creator?

We "Beings" are the Seeds of the Creator!

"Beings" are destined to evolve into Co-Creator's to help
create life throughout the infinitely expanding cosmos.

This is the Grand Cycle of Aquarius,
Cosmic Consciousness Creating Pure Altruistic
Manifesting "Light Beings."

"You will return whence you came;"
Conscious to Consciousness

Part V

Psychological War Fare

In this section I am simply exercising **my** freedom of speech to share Rational thoughts, and to provoke some critical, thinking, before its game over!

As I was about to release this book the virus scam-demic struck the world and simultaneously the world economic crisis began to unfold, just as I had perceived.

The Armageddon is secretly underway, psychological warfare has been unleashed upon the masses. We need to get into an offensive mode!

Remember, FEAR is the ultimate weapon utilized by the secret society, or ruling elite, to control mankind. What better way to ensue world Fear than to exploit the common cold, or re-named corona virus, as a pandemic in order to relinquish humanity of what remaining rights we have left?

For almost a year on end, they broadcast 24/7 the infected and death numbers in world media, newsprint, and radio. This is Fear broadcasting, Psychological warfare!. In fact, the so called covid-19 virus has not realistically claimed any more of the already unhealthy and elderly than the renamed common cold did in 2019. Suicide, cancer, alcoholism, drugs, wars, and starvation, individually kill more people every year, than covid-19. Why are these deaths not broadcast 24/7. How many "Beings" are slaughtered daily by the elites war machine? In the first six months of 2020, elicit drugs killed 78% more people in British Columbia Canada than the covid-19. The homicide rate for native women in northern Canada is 4.82 deaths per 1000, while covid-19 is less than 0.3 deaths per 1000. Every year more than ten million people are literally starved to death, thats twenty five thousand daily, ten times more deaths than covid-19, and starvation is expected to double this year because of the lockdowns. Car accidents claim more lives than covid-19. You have a greater chance of being killed in your vehicle, than dying from covid-19. Governments claim the lockdowns are to save lives, but obviously their priorities are disturbingly distorted. Think Rationally!

The common cold has been with us every spring and fall since the beginning of civilization, and it mutates every year while we "Beings" build natural immunity to it year after year. It is Creations merciful way of assisting the sick and elderly to quickly pass when it is their time, rather than a prolonged induced suffering from pharmaceutical chemicals, radiation treatment, and comatose life support. Secondly, older people are a rapidly growing portion of the world population, so the death toll will increases substantially each year also, right! This is Creation working its magical balancing act with all life, ensuring only the strong and healthy survive. We can't and shouldn't, control Creation!

FEAR broadcasting 24/7 is forced-mind programming, mind control just like the Muslim religious broadcasting I mention in my earlier, this is psychological warfare! The ruling elite force "Beings" to believe their dictated deception. The ultimate goal is to force "Beings" to submit to deceptive laws through Fear, while incrementally relinquishing all human rights and freedom to implement a NWO. It is now illegal for friends, families, and communities to gather. Dictated social distance laws prevent "Beings" from voicing or communicating or protesting social injustices and human rights violations.

They are now driving wedges between every faucet of humanity, between families and freinds. They want to divide everyone in order to prevent the masses from uniting in protest. And the true intent of disarming citizens is to prevent any resistance to the enforcement of a totalitarian system. They want us to play in their major league with sticks and stones.

Programmed Fear has driven perfectly strong, healthy people to self-imprison by locking themselves in their home with a bottle of sanitizer, trembling in Fear. If this were in fact a deadly virus, then why do they tell people who feel sick to simply quarantine yourself for 14 days, and all's well, no need to go to the hospital? This is psychological war fare!

Thinking Rationally one would consider the alternative, and say; Stop, Enough is Enough. The broadcast mortality rate of covid -19 worldwide is about 3. Mortality rates are disclosed as 1 per 1000, or in this case, an equivalent of 0.3 %, meaning that a healthy "Being" has a 99.7% chance of survival! Think about this Rationally, you have a 99.7% opportunity to continue living life to its fullest. Submitting to forced lockdowns, masks, and vaccines with these odds is fear driven madness, insanity.

It is psychological warfare!

Think! What is more live threatening, than covid-19. Picture, looking down the dim muzzle of a Nuclear silo, only to see the tip of a war head pointed at your head, simultaneously the dim glare of a dark red light, suddenly starts flashing bright amber. How fast do you respond? BAHAAA; Hit the "Emergency Stop", Right! The world is this close to nuclear war! But yet you fear covid-19 more, Why?

Well consider the following before hiding in your closet trembling in fear, awaiting some deceptive magic vaccine.

Covid has a kill rate of 3 people per 1000 or 99.7% survival rate,. Cancer has a kill rate of 166 per 1000 or 83 % survival rate. The 5G system will accelerate cancers deaths to approx. 332 per 1000 leaving less than a 70% survival rate. Comparing the leading causes of death globally, their are literally fifty plus categories with ten to twenty times higher mortality rates than covid-19. Nuclear war has the potential to destroy all life, and our planet, but we fear covid-19 most, Why?

This is not Rational thinking! It is programmed fear without thought. This is psychological warfare being applied!

Apparently covid-19, may have mutated from a bat. Over six hundred thousand mink have been destroyed in Europe over covid-19. And in Spain as of July 16 2020, they plan on destroying ninety thousand mink because 87% of them have covid-19. My initial though was, Wow! but they're all still alive and healthy? How irrational is this. Another irrational fact is that 80 to 90% of the world population have also contracted covid-19 while showing no symptoms and are still alive and healthy. So why the lockdown, why the mask, and why is mandatory testing and a magic vaccine required, when the majority of the masses have obviously already built a natural immunity to it, just like the mink!

Furthermore, humans, mink, and bats, clarify that mammals do contract and transmit pandemic-causing viruses and bacteria to humans, right. So what about our pets, and livestock and other wildlife? What about mosquitos', flies and insects, they are also known carriers and transmitters of diseases and viruses. Rational thought would conclude that social distancing laws, are simply a form of psychological war fare and pathetically redundant.

Rational thought would further conclude that the primary purpose of the lockdown and social distancing laws is to make AI mass surveillance more proficient in the surveillance, identification, profiling, and tracking of the masses, and to hunt and target individual or group resistance, and to accustom the masses to the new norm of totalitarianizm. I believe the true purpose of lockdowns is to force the masses into submission and compliance, in order to incrementally relinquish all human rights.

The overuse of sanitizers has been long known to weaken the immune system. Stress and depression are known to drastically weaken the immune system. And the 5G system deteriorates the immune system on a cellular level. Independent health professionals know this, but are censored and totally ignored, so what's really going on? Our political puppets attempt to enforce dictated laws from the elite, which are known to weaken our immune systems, then dictate that everyone must take some evil vaccine, without our consent or knowledge of its true formula or its true intent.

For decades, Bill Gates has been the primary proponent of world depopulation. He has a documented track record of killer vaccines, but now hypocritically insisting that everyone must be vaccinated with his vaccine to save lives. Simultaneously ten million people are starving to death, while governments spend trillions of dollars developing weapons to slaughter people, more efficiently! This reeks of deception Billy. What's the true intention of deliberately destroying the masses immune systems, and making the masses more susceptible. What happens when natures cold virus mutates again? It will most definitely kill multiple times more elderly next year. Is this the underlying intent, to exterminate as many elderly as possible? After all, our aging population is a huge costs burden to governments, like acute and long term health care needs, pension payouts, hospitals beds, medications, care homes, transportation, etc. These are a rapidly increasing costs burden as the world population approach retirement age. Are the none productive elderly, the primary target of this sinister plot?

The ruling elite know they will meet resistance from a greater percentage of the masses by implementing NWO. Do some critical thinking with an open mind to all possibilities and ask: what if covid-19 and the vaccine are in fact a deception? Whereby the vaccine would protect the programmed obedient sheep accepting the Nano-chip serum from a pre-engineered deadly virus to be released upon the non-compliant masses. What if the mandatory testing for covid-19's true intent is to obtain everyone's DNA to be utilized for genetic cleansing, genetic mutation or trans-humanism? Thinking rationally, producing trans-human slave robot's, and terminating the non-compliant is a logical cost efficient way to depopulate, assimilate, control, and enslave civilization. Do the Borg's from television's Star Trek series come to mind? AI biotechnology is in fact beyond this stage! Watch this U-tub; Human 2.0, A wake up call to the World by Dr. Carrie Madej.

Perhaps this entire deceptive exercise is a test; a feeler gauge, testing the limitations of the masses before resistance ignites, and to determine what addition measures are required prior to implementing a total lock down when the system is switched over to AI. What if the exploitation of covid-19 deaths is a distraction utilized to absorb the blame for increased deaths caused by excessive 5G radiation.

My point is that the ruling elite have masterminded a strategic military plan for (NOW), and will attempt to implement it by any means necessary, including psychological war fare. They have no morals or conscience whatsoever. They will slaughter billions to achieve their sinister desires. The US and its allies are presently threatening the world with nuclear enforcement if their desires aren't met. This is shear "Evil Insanity", "Madness", driven by infinite greed and lust for world dominance. It must be Stopped!

Why has the USA got the worst scenario of covid-19 in the world while having the least congested population compared to many other countries with lower living standards? Perhaps the death count is a fabricated deception, utilized to institute marshal law and destroy the American constitution. The US constitution presents the greatest obstacle to the implementation of NWO.

Enough is Enough! The ruling elite have no more right than any individual to all the lands and resources. They have absolutely no right to our souls and our bodies. We did not consent to being enslaved at birth, we did not consent their dictated laws, and constant wars. We did not consent to their lockdown. And I believe that the majority of "Beings" will not consent to an unknown evil vaccine. All "Beings" have a birthright to freedom and right of free choice!

The masses must unite as one collective force, with one common goal, and that is to take back control of our world before we are all totally enslaved, or our planet is totally destroyed.

Enough is Enough! It is time for Change!

Sports, however entertaining; are an elaborate distraction to the world reality rapidly unfolding. Civilization has entered the cusp of a new dawn. and the Real Armageddon has been silently initiated with the masses totally unaware. "Being" vs NWO is in progress and the present score is nada for "Beings". The winner of this world event determines civilization's destiny. It is an Armageddon without rules.

But the ruling elite has overlooked the masses programmed love of competitive sport and our programmed will to win. We are programmed to provide unrivaled support for our preferred Team. We need to utilize their pre-programming to our advantage! Sports fans; we are the greater majority of the world masses, and the most powerful avenue to initiate a tsunami wave of support for Team "Beings".

Team "Beings" are the key to salvation, we must prevail in this Armageddon. We are 7.5 billion strong, and collectively, we "Beings" are the most powerful, unstoppable force on Earth. But we must unite as one collective force, with one common goal, before its game over!

One by One, "Team Being" Fans Awaken!

Two by Two "Team Being" Fans Unite Worldwide.

United, "Team Being" Fans manifest a Tsunami Wave of support that ripples across the globe.

Collectively Team "Beings" manifest positive world change for the greater good of all live!

IT IS CREATIONS WILL, AND OUR DESTINY.

I am very grateful for awakening to share this knowledge and understanding with "All Fellow Beings". However, time is of critical essence. Man has reached the final and most critical fork on civilizations path. It is time to make a Choice for Change. We have suffered in negative energy for two thousand years, it is time for "Beings" to thrive in positive enregy.

One by One, we must assimilate and
unite the collective force.

We must manifest the Most Powerful
Force on Earth: "Love Energy"

Believe in "Being", believe in Beings power.

Embraces this inevitable evolutionary
change with love for all life.

May the force be with you and loved ones.

Please share this book worldwide to initiate the collective power of "Team "Being."

Shop and wear "Team Being" Sports apparel. Display your collective status to the world; visit us at teambeings.ca

References

A perception of Worldly Truths derived from consciousness after conducting 35 years of research on a broad area of topics, which are to numerous to list. The intention of this knowledge and understanding was to share it eniquivically with “All Fellow Beings”. This is Creations Will.

Words of Wisdom

The secret to freedom lies in educating people, the secret of tranny is keeping them ignorant, (Maximilien Robespierre)

Faith is to believe that which you do not yet see; and the reward of this faith is to see that which you believe.
Saint Augustine of Hippo (354-430)

The mind acts like an enemy for those who don't control and correct their thoughts.

Respond intelligently even to unintellegent treatment. La Tzu (Cica 6th centruy BC)

Hate is not conquered by Hate, Hate is conquered by Love, This is the Law eternal. (Gautama Budda (563-483 BC)

CPSIA information can be obtained
at www.ICGtesting.com
Printed in the USA
LVHW011945131220
674086LV00024B/647

9 780228 837848